1997

CROSSING
CULTURES
THROUGH FILM

CROSSING CULTURES THROUGH FILM

ELLEN SUMMERFIELD

INTERCULTURAL PRESS, INC.

For information, contact:
Intercultural Press, Inc.
P.O. Box 700
Yarmouth, Maine 04096, USA

Book design and production by Patty J. Topel
Cover design by Ralph Copeland

Printed in the United States of America

97   96   2   3   4   5   6   7

Library of Congress Cataloging-in-Publication Data

Summerfield, Ellen
  Crossing cultures through film/Ellen Summerfield.
    p. cm.
  Includes bibliographical references and index.
  ISBN 1-877864-21-8
  1. Intercultural communication in motion pictures. 2. Minorities in motion pictures. 3. Racism in motion pictures. I. Title.

PN 1995.9.I55S86   1993
791.43'655—dc20   93-10456
                                             CIP

Contents

Preface

At the heart of efforts in the academy to promote diversity and to work toward multicultural and international curricula is the clear-sighted recognition that we must find new ways to relate to our fellow human beings. In our own neighborhoods and on the planet as a whole, our very survival seems now to hinge on our ability to find new approaches, to learn new skills, and to create new metaphors. Traditionally held definitions no longer apply, and exisiting theories seem less and less workable. Indeed, the definition of ourselves as a people—as Americans—is undergoing persistent revision, our national history is being reinterpreted and rewritten, and our view of our role in the world community is changing dramatically.

The present work grew out of this atmosphere of questioning and soul-searching in the university. Over the years, I have seen the power of cross-cultural films in the classroom and in workshops but have found little direction available on how to use them effectively. This book is intended to help provide that direction to international and intercultural educators in a number of different fields: ethnic studies, anthropology, communication, education, English as a second language, history, international business, and foreign languages. The book also addresses the needs of international student advisors and of study abroad coordinators, as well as of cross-cultural trainers in business and the community. While *Crossing Cultures through Film* is aimed at university and adult educators, high school teachers should find it of interest as well.

Because I am looking at what happens when people from different cultures come into contact, films that examine a single culture in isolation, such as National Geographic specials, are not included. I do, however, discuss a number of films that look at how a particular subculture functions within the larger society. I have not defined "culture" in its broadest terms, but have concentrated on differences of nationality, race, and ethnicity. Other cultural divisions based on gender, age, physical ability, class, sexual orientation, and religion, can also be explored in film, but are not of primary interest here. My focus on three cultural boundaries does not mean to deny the simple truth that in any interaction there may be several other variables at play. Furthermore, much of what is said about nationality, race, and ethnicity could apply as well to other groups separated by more or less clearly defined differences.

In selecting films for discussion, I have tried to include a variety of different cultural groups in contact with each other. I did not make an attempt to be comprehensive. More important to me than comprehensiveness are the pedagogical methods described, for they can be applied to films about any cross-cultural interaction.

While working on the book, I was often aware that I was writing from my own cultural perspective, that of a white American woman. Being inevitably trapped inside this perspective, I realize that I am not able to see the whole picture. I offer film interpretations from my one vantage point and write in the expectation that educators with other insights and other points of view will help to illuminate areas that may not have been visible to me.

Because I believe that pedagogy is best when it is concrete, I have included as examples many of my own experiences with cross-cultural films. Most of the examples come from my teaching, but some also come from my observations over the past few years as a student in workshops and seminars. The "Tips for Use," which have grown out of my personal experiences using the films in question, are intended to provide additional ideas for discussion, journal writing, field work, and, in some cases, reading assignments. The Tips are meant to serve as examples of the types of exercises facilitators may wish to develop. They are not included for all films discussed, but many of the Tips suggested for one particular film can be modified to apply to others as well.

With regard to terminology, I have used the terms "film" and "video" (or "videotape") interchangeably. Since almost all of the films discussed in the book are also available in video (VHS) format, the distinction between the two did not seem important. I have not provided information on availability of films in various formats (16mm, 3/4 U-Matic, VHS, Beta) but am assuming that most educators are using VHS.

At the end of the chapters, I have provided information on how to obtain the films for rental or purchase. In the case of documentaries, which may be available from multiple sources, I have simply given the name of one primary distributor (addresses are provided at the end of the book). Since feature films can be rented or purchased most easily from local video stores— or from film clubs such as Facets Multimedia and Home Film Festival—I have provided sources only for feature films that might be difficult to locate. The information is as current as possible, but film distributors tend to change their offerings— and their addresses—quite frequently. With the help of the reference materials described in chapter 2, however, it should not be difficult to track down a film.

In the course of my research, a number of people involved in film and media have generously shared their time and expertise with me. I would especially like to thank Cornelius Moore of California Newsreel, John Rowe of Filmakers Library, Michael Jeung of NAATA, Kym Ragusa of Third World Newsreel, Mai King of Women Make Movies, and James Lee of First Run/Icarus for their kind assistance. For allowing me to spend extended periods of time in their media center previewing rooms and sharing their ideas with me, I am very grateful to Mary Nelson and Donald Bartholomew of the University of Washington Extension Media Services and Charlotte Earle of the University of California Extension Media Service. My sincere thanks as well to Joanne Hamilton and the staff at the Portland State University Continuing Education Film and Video Library, to the staff at the Intercultural Communication Institute, and to Diane Harris of Foundation for Global Community in Portland, Oregon.

I further wish to express my appreciation to Linfield College for approving a sabbatical leave for me in 1990-91 for the purpose of writing this book. The staff of Linfield's Northup Library—Lynn Chmelir, Frances Rasmussen, and Susan Whyte—have been extremely helpful to me throughout this project, and I am especially grateful to Sue DeHut of Educational Media Services for her able assistance. For moral support and many useful suggestions, I thank my colleagues Rosario Aglialoro, Sandra Lee, Tom Love, Annette Schoof, and Sandy Soohoo-Refaei, and I also wish to thank student assistants Ada Adamor and Kiersten Marsh.

As this book evolved, I had the good fortune to be enrolled in two summer seminars taught by experts in the use of film in cross-cultural communication. I am indebted both to the late Dean Barnlund (San Francisco State University) and to John Condon (University of New Mexico) for sharing a wealth of knowledge about film in these seminars and for providing ideas and inspiration.

My thanks to my parents, Helene and Powell Summerfield, who for years have alerted me to anything cross-cultural on television. To my friend and colleague, Kareen Sturgeon, my deepest thanks for critical readings of the manuscript at several stages and for our invaluable conversations on pedagogy. From the beginning of this work to its conclusion, Phillip Pirages has assisted me in countless ways. I cannot thank him enough for his sensitive, skillful editing of the entire manuscript and his support and encouragement throughout.

For their expert assistance and very humane ways, I express my appreciation to Toby Frank, Ben Gross, David Hoopes, and Peggy Pusch of the Intercultural Press.

Finally, I wish to extend a special word of thanks to the students who have helped me learn about film and whose thoughts and responses have been incorporated throughout this book.

1

Why Films?: Creating a Cross-Cultural Laboratory

This book could not have been written ten years ago. The video revolution has dramatically changed the ways in which film can now be incorporated into our teaching. Because of the ready availability of videos, educators now have easy access to thousands of films and documentaries, many of which are relatively inexpensive. Video stores can be found in even the smallest towns, and educators can purchase video recorders, making it possible to tape their own materials. Given this incredibly rich new resource, what is its value as a tool for cross-cultural learning? How might it best be used? What can it do for us?

Film helps to create a unique environment for cross-cultural learning because it speaks to our emotions as well as our intellect. Learning about stereotypes, ethnocentrism, discrimination, and acculturation in the abstract can be flat and uninspiring. But if we *experience* intercultural contact with our eyes and ears, we begin to understand it. Although watching the film *Arab and Jew* (page 96) is admittedly not the same as living in Israel and experiencing the situation firsthand, viewing the film allows us to enter into this world and feel its conflicts; we can almost believe we have lived certain events ourselves.

Another advantage of film is that it provides entry into topics that seem too controversial, too uncomfortable for many educators to handle in other ways. Film breaks through barriers, giving students permission to do the same; as they think and talk about a film, they are of course really talking about themselves—but in a form that is indirect and, thus, relatively safe. A film such as *Racism 101* (page 115), for example, which addresses black-white relations in forthright terms, helps students overcome their own inhibitions

1

or hesitation to talk about racial issues. They gain confidence in their ability to express themselves on sensitive matters; they can test their views and begin to learn how others think and react.

Consequently, film serves as a catalyst, creating interactions between cultures on the screen and, at the same time, in the audience. Through this mixing of cultures, the classroom becomes a genuine laboratory, a testing ground which offers protection from injury but does not allow things to stay as they are. As educators use film to create this laboratory, what is it that they are hoping to achieve? If the goal is defined as learning to interact with each other across cultures in ways that are more peaceable, just, and enriching, how can film help achieve this goal?

Film proves to be particularly effective in three areas of cross-cultural learning. First, film study enables students to recognize and unlearn stereotypes. Since film produces and reinforces stereotypes, the analysis of film is an excellent way to learn how stereotypes operate. As students begin to recognize a particular stereotype and see how it influences them, they become less susceptible to manipulation. In our age of mass media, it is doubly important to create opportunities for students to become critical viewers and listeners. (Chapter 5 will focus on the topic of stereotypes in film, and the subject will recur in discussions of specific films elsewhere in the book.)

Second, film helps students recognize how cultures differ in verbal and nonverbal patterns of communication. In real life, there is no opportunity to replay an interaction. As people speculate on why communication may have succeeded or failed, they must rely on their often inaccurate memory. With film, however, scenes can be replayed repeatedly for the purpose of careful analysis. Students can observe how words, gestures, facial expressions, eye contact, intonation, and silences are all tied to culture. For many students, this type of analysis may be totally new; as they dissect and reflect on the interactions on screen, they will become sensitized to patterns of communication within their own cultural group as well as across cultures. (While chapter 6 deals specifically with how to use film to understand nonverbal and verbal communication, this theme, like that of stereotypes, runs through many discussions in the book.)

Third, film can be used as a powerful tool to help students develop empathy, a response that has been widely recognized as critical to successful cross-cultural interactions. Empathy is generally defined as the ability to experience the other person's point of view, to comprehend the other's feelings, thoughts, and motives. Film helps us to develop empathy by causing us to identify with certain characters, to feel their emotions. In the film *Witness* (page 147), for example, an encounter between the Amish protagonists and a group of Sunday tourists illustrates the indignity of being photographed as a curiosity. Since we see the events from the Amish point of view, we feel their annoyance and embarrassment and are put off by the crude behavior of the tourists. If we have never before thought of how it might feel to be the object of voyeuristic attention because of our culture, this scene serves to help sensitize us.

The premise underlying the pedagogy of the entire book is that learning will be translated into commitments. Showing a film is only the beginning; through follow-up discussions and activities, students can discover their own cross-cultural interests and their own direction. Exactly where the new ideas and interests will ultimately lead is generally not apparent at the outset. What is important, however, is that students begin to see how the challenges and rewards of cross-cultural learning are relevant to their own lives. A great deal is accomplished if they are motivated to learn more about other peoples and cultures and if they begin to take responsible action as a result.

The types of personal action that might follow from new insights may seem quite modest. One police captain who took my class in intercultural communication, for example, decided to order a copy of the film *A Class Divided* (page 50) for his department and to schedule an in-service workshop around it. For a number of students, the most immediate practical result of their learning has been to talk to a person from a different culture whom they had been reluctant to approach. An American student wrote that after watching *Racism 101*, he overcame his hesitation to join a group of international students at a lunch table in the dining hall. Another student working in a large corporation wrote that the films from the *Going International* series (page 152) helped him realize that he had misjudged a colleague from Singapore; he subsequently made an effort to clear up some misunderstandings that had arisen between them.

But these seemingly small steps are actually breakthroughs, and they empower students to continue their cross-cultural exploration. We are not so much aiming to change the world as we are to bring change into our particular part of it. Once people realize that they have the means to make concrete changes in their own lives, the implications are profound and liberating.

Noticeably missing from the above discussion is the idea of transmitting *information* through film. Undeniably, film can be used effectively for this purpose—for instance, to instruct about the religions of India or the history of China. However, because the mere possession of factual knowledge does not necessarily bring with it personal involvement or commitment, the pedagogy of this book is not primarily concerned with gaining information about other cultures through film. Of course, commitment and interest must, in the long run, go together with a solid base of knowledge. There is no doubt that thorough knowledge of another culture— its history, language, arts, religion, economics, politics—is fundamental to harmonious long-term relations. But I am relying on film to stimulate this kind of learning more than to provide it. Once students become involved with another culture, they will find their own ways to pursue their interests. Of course, you can also direct their attention to ideas for further study, examples of which will be given throughout the book.

While the three uses of film as discussed above—to unlearn stereotypes, to recognize different patterns of communication, and to develop empathy—are given primary emphasis here, you will no doubt find other forms of intercultural learning taking place as a result of your own use of film. Films can promote everything from a basic excitement and curiosity about other cultures to a deep sense of a shared fate with peoples of the world—a sense of the interconnectedness of life and of the need for cooperation across all boundaries of cultural difference to achieve common goals.

2

An Embarrassment of Riches: How to Find and Evaluate Films

If you are interested in using films in your classroom, workshop, or seminar but have never done so before, the first obvious task is to locate appropriate sources for rental or purchase. In this age of mass media, we are blessed with an abundance of possibilities. Recent technology has given us easy access to a wealth of materials from television and the movie industry. The major difficulty, it seems, is not so much finding, but rather choosing from, a wide variety of materials from around the world.

Where to Locate Audiovisuals

In this book, approximately fifty films are discussed in some detail, and another hundred or so are mentioned within the text or in annotated lists at the end of chapters. This group should provide a good starting point for your search or, if you are already using films, should offer some new ideas.

Natural places to find these films—and many more—are nearby public and university libraries. Most libraries now have their own audiovisual collections as well as media reference books and catalogues. You may be surprised at how many useful materials are available in local libraries at little or no cost.

If you are interested primarily in audiovisual rentals, you will want to familiarize yourself with catalogues from some of the large college and university media centers around the country, where rental fees for a videocassette usually range from $15 to $25. Since some centers are more expensive than others, you will benefit from comparative pricing. Addresses of several media centers with fine cross-cultural collections—including the University of Washington, the University of California Extension Media Center, Syracuse University, Indiana University, and the University of Illinois—are provided at the end of the book.

A more comprehensive list of addresses is found in the *Educational Film and Video Locator* (fourth edition), an invaluable reference work which provides descriptions and locations of nearly 52,000 films and videos available at the forty-six member institutions of the national Consortium of College and University Media Centers. Assuming that you already have a title, the Locator will tell you where it can be obtained for rental. If you are searching for a particular kind of film, the *Locator*'s index categorizes audiovisuals according to subject headings such as "Acculturation," "Blacks," "Civil Rights," "Ethnic Groups," and "Immigration and Emigration."

The most useful reference work for purchase rather than rental information is *Bowker's Complete Video Directory 1992*. Bowker's first volume contains 35,000 entertainment and performance titles, and the second volume contains 52,000 special-interest and educational videos. An index of Spanish-language films lists several thousand titles.

A computer database called A-V Online provides comprehensive references to nonprint educational media, including 16mm films, videotapes, filmstrips, and other formats. A-V Online is produced by the National Information Center for Educational Media (NICEM), is distributed by Access Innovations, Inc. in Albuquerque, New Mexico, and is updated on a quarterly basis. You might check to see if your library has access to it through the Dialog Information Retrieval Service. However, you should be aware that there is an hourly service charge as well as a fee to print each citation.

A valuable directory of films and videos on international and cross-cultural issues is Lee Zeigler's *Film and Video Resources for International Educational Exchange*. Zeigler provides capsule descriptions of over 250 items, many of which have been produced by university-based faculty and staff. Another extremely useful guide to multicultural video is Barbara Abrash and Catherine Egan's

Mediating History, which focuses on independent productions by and about African-American, Asian-American, Latino, and Native-American people. Though intended for historians, the book is a wonderful resource for any educator interested in seeing how these four groups portray their own histories on film. (Complete references to these and similar sources of information cited in the text are provided in the Selected Bibliography.)

As organizations increasingly begin to establish their own video libraries, many with lending privileges, you may find materials in unexpected places. Foreign consulates often publish lists of materials which are usually available at no cost. Professional organizations such as the Northeast Conference on the Teaching of Foreign Languages and NAFSA: Association of International Educators also provide lists of available videos. Depending on your interests, you might try historical societies, museums, peace groups, and community groups. In Portland, Oregon, for example, Educators for Social Responsibility, Physicians for Social Responsibility, and Foundation for Global Community/Beyond War make audiovisual materials available, as do the Oregon International Council in Salem and the organization Mobility International USA in Eugene.[1]

You may also wish to obtain catalogues and be placed on mailing lists of distributors and production companies which offer cross-cultural films for rental or purchase. A selected list of these companies is provided at the end of the book. Of special interest is the National Film Board of Canada, which has long been working to foster Canada's national policy of multiculturalism and which produces outstanding films, including many shorts. Also noteworthy is NAATA/CrossCurrent Media, which produces excellent audiovisual materials on Asian Americans. California Newsreel has superb special collections on African cinema, Southern Africa and antiapartheid, and black America. Filmakers Library, First Run/Icarus Films, and PBS Video have extensive catalogues with large selections of exceptional cross-cultural audiovisuals. Women Make Movies offers many fine films by and about women of color from around the world. Finally, Third World Newsreel makes available notable collections such as "Palestinian Voices," "Latin American Voices," "Voices from the African Diaspora," and "Voices from the Asian Diaspora."

A marvelous source for rental and purchase of videos is Facets Multimedia Center in Chicago. Facets produces a catalogue of almost 17,000 foreign, classic American, silent, documentary, fine arts, and children's videos. By calling a toll-free number, you can order films for rental at approximately $10 each, plus return postage. Most of the videos listed are also available for purchase. Other video clubs, such as Home Film Festival, offer similar services.

Lastly, a source not to be overlooked is your local video store. In most larger cities, there are video stores which specialize in classic and foreign films. These can be gold mines of material from around the world. In chain stores and smaller local outlets, many useful materials can be found as well. Moreover, local video stores are usually willing to order videotapes for you.

Making or Taping Your Own Materials

You may wish to supplement materials available for loan, rental, or purchase with your own off-air videotapes or homemade productions. These two options lend spontaneity and immediacy to your presentations, allowing you to incorporate the most up-to-date materials and to address matters of concern in your own classroom or community.

With regard to taping your own materials off the air from broadcast or cable television, you need to be aware of copyright law, which continues to change as new technology is developed and new questions are posed and interpreted. The information most important for educators is contained in Esther R. Sinofsky's *Off-Air Videotaping in Education*. The guidelines that apply to nonprofit educational institutions stipulate that off-air tapes of broadcast and cable television (excluding pay cable, pay television, and Instructional Television Fixed Service) may be retained for forty-five days after the air date, but must be erased at the end of forty-five days unless permission to keep the program is sought from the creator or a licensing agreement is signed. During the first ten consecutive school days in the forty-five-day period, the recording may be shown once in each class "in the course of relevant teaching activities" and repeated "once only when instructional reinforcement is necessary."[2]

Thus, the majority of television broadcasts—whether dramas and sitcoms, talk shows, educational programs, or news—can be taped under fair-use guidelines for one-time presentation to your classes. Should you decide that the material is important enough to be saved, you can write for permission or follow procedures for licensing. Standard copyright books often contain form letters for such procedures, or you can consult the media specialist at your university.

Of particular value are segments from talk shows like those conducted by Phil Donahue and Oprah Winfrey and segments from television newsmagazines such as 60 *Minutes*. Many multicultural issues are addressed on these shows, from hate crimes to affirmative action. The talk shows have the advantage of presenting a wide spectrum of opinions as audience members interact with guest presenters.

Increasingly, multicultural issues are being introduced into prime-time television series. In the past few seasons, the three major networks have all offered new series in which race is central to the story, and cable networks are doing the same. You can turn as well to established dramas and sitcoms for evidence of multicultural topics. A long-running lawyer drama, for example, included such topics during a recent season in seven of its twenty-two episodes, the most memorable of which was the custody battle between a white mother and a Native American father, which was settled in a Navajo court. Relevant segments from current television shows not only provide interesting material for use in discussing cross-cultural issues, but also reveal how the mass media are treating them.

Clips from news broadcasts also demonstrate the relevance of cross-cultural issues in our daily life. For example, when we were studying the concept of cultural literacy, I showed my class a discussion taped from *The MacNeil/Lehrer NewsHour* involving E. D. Hirsch, the author of *Cultural Literacy*, along with author Maya Angelou, psychologist Robert Coles, and a high school teacher. The students were fascinated to see that "abstract" issues were causing such heated debate on the evening news.

Homemade videos also serve to bridge the gap between theoretical and real-life concerns. In ESL classes, for example, I have observed students acting out role plays featuring different cross-cultural interactions, such as an international student asking an American student for a date, asking a professor for help, or dealing with a roommate problem. The interactions were videotaped, and students then analyzed them in terms of differing values, perceptions, and modes of communication. Any of the role plays suggested in subsequent chapters could be videotaped and used in this way. They also can be saved and shown to other groups. For example, a segment on the difficulties international students have in American classrooms could be shown to professors.

In his article, "Defusing Tensions with Film: A Way Away from Racial Polarizations," Bernard S. Miller describes another intriguing use of self-made videotapes. As a means of dealing with severe racial tensions at Hunter College High School in New York, the faculty and administration decided to film a series of small-group discussions on the topic, "What It Means to Be a Black or Puerto Rican at Hunter." Student participants in the various discussions soon began to talk freely and openly, forgetting about the camera. From more than two hours of discussions, a twenty-minute program was edited and shown to faculty at a day-long race relations conference and also to classes. Miller says that the film had a "tremendous" impact. Students and teachers were more attentive "in a darkened room than in a large lighted assembly hall where compelling distractions abound." He adds that "when the people in the film are fellow students dealing with live issues, the motivation to pay attention is virtually guaranteed."[3]

Another ambitious project for videotaping is to write and perform a play on cross-cultural issues. For example, Linfield College administrator Joette Rose, with funding from NAFSA's Cooperative Grants

Program, wrote a play entitled A Letter Home, which deals with students' adjustments to living and studying abroad. The play was performed throughout the state of Oregon and was videotaped for classroom use.

Evaluating Films and Videos

As we begin to locate and preview cross-cultural films, questions arise as to how to evaluate them. What criteria might we use to determine their quality and suitability? What are our standards and expectations? On what basis might we find a film objectionable? Or decide to reject it?

The place to begin is with the interests and needs of your particular group. Is the content of the film appropriate for your group? Is the film too basic? Too specialized? While some films, such as the classics discussed in chapter 4, can be shown to practically any group, others need to be used more selectively, depending on the content and level of difficulty. While a class in Japanese language or Asian history might find the cross-cultural perspectives in The Go Masters fascinating, the film is too specialized and demanding for a freshman orientation session on diversity. Certain films might be too advanced linguistically for an ESL class, while others might not be appropriate in content for the needs of international students. Many film catalogues indicate suggested age levels from kindergarten and preschool through college and adult. Clearly, the fit needs to be determined from the outset.

In addition to judging suitability of content and level, you must decide if your group is emotionally prepared to handle films which deal with sensitive, controversial issues. If you do not yet know a group well enough to judge possible reactions, you should start with less sensitive materials. The sequencing of multicultural materials is of paramount importance, and it is almost always advisable to begin more conservatively and then move to more controversial areas. Once a sense of trust develops among group members, and between yourself and the group, you can venture into more challenging territory. Without this trust, it is very risky to plunge into highly charged areas of prejudice and racism.

Are there any films that are inadvisable to use with even a mature group? This is a matter of your own judgment and discretion. Personally, I tend to avoid films that are excessively violent, out of a conviction that watching violence on the screen tends to sensationalize more than to sensitize. Thus I would reject a film such as Mario Van Peeble's *New Jack City*, for, whatever its other virtues may be, it overflows with gratuitous bloodshed and brutality.

Also, once in a while I decide to reject a film because it seems too oppressive, too depressing. An example of this for me is the 1967 film *Where Is Prejudice?*, which documents a dispiriting week-long workshop retreat of twelve college students of different ethnic backgrounds and religious faiths. At the outset, all twelve deny being prejudiced, and indeed they seem to be open-minded, liberal types of the sixties mold. What happens in just a week is profoundly disturbing: deep, seemingly unbridgeable hostilities surface, and a near total breakdown of relations occurs. The film ends with no resolution and leaves the viewers in a mood of hopelessness.

The question of whether to show a film of this nature goes to the heart of our professional ethics. Undeniably, in this field we need to confront harsh realities. It would be irresponsible to gloss over prejudices or minimize the difficulties of cross-cultural communication. But it would seem that, even in the interest of truth, it is equally unethical for us as multicultural educators to strip away hope. The argument in favor of using *Where Is Prejudice?* is that it is so shocking and powerful as to provide a depth of understanding found virtually nowhere else. Some multicultural educators, including myself, have found that it left an unforgettable impresssion and was beneficial in shaping their views. In considering whether to provide this type of intense learning experience, you should carefully assess the maturity of the group and avoid showing the film in a final lesson. There needs to be ample time to process the students' reactions and to provide more hopeful outlooks.

On the other end of the spectrum, intriguing questions arise in evaluating cross-cultural materials that are lighthearted and humorous in approach. When is humor objectionable, and when is it salutary? People may be willing to poke fun at their own ethnic, racial, or national group, but they can easily become defensive when outsiders do the same. Because reactions to humor are unpredictable, caution is always advisable. On the other hand, how can we ever expect to succeed at cross-cultural work if, out of fear of offending, we abandon humor?

A case in point is the 1986 video entitled *Gung Ho* (page 161), which some people find hilarious, others tasteless. *Gung Ho* shows the cultural clashes that follow when a Japanese auto firm reopens a failed factory in an American rust-belt city. Both Americans and Japanese are spoofed, at times to the point of absurdity. A colleague in ESL has used the film for several years with groups of largely Japanese students, and she reports that they enjoy it immensely. Another colleague in Japan says that while her Japanese students find parts of it to be offensive, they nevertheless regard it as instructive and worthwhile.

A final criterion for evaluation has to do with geographic relevance. Depending on where you live, you might find certain films and videos particularly interesting and appropriate. In Oregon, for example, the film *River People: Behind the Case of David Sohappy* (page 73) has special meaning, since Sohappy's struggle for fishing rights took place along the Columbia River. I first saw this film at the Northwest Film and Video Center in Portland with an audience of about two hundred people. The emotion in the room was intense, especially when landscapes beloved to Oregonians were shown as the scene of conflict and controversy. Other films in my Oregon collection include *Old Believers*, which focuses on the Russian Orthodox community in the small town of Woodburn, and *Moving Mountains*, a look at a group of Yiu Mien refugees who settled in Portland. You will probably want to be on the lookout for films specific to your own region, not only because students find them relevant, but because follow-up activities can include field work linked directly to the film.

Assessing Biases and Factual Accuracy

One of the most difficult problems we face is how to evaluate films and videos for accuracy and reliability in depictions of cultures. How can we know if a film portrays a culture in ways that are superficial, distorted, or blatantly inaccurate? How can we recognize a film that is the product of in-depth knowledge of a culture and respect for its complexities? In some cases, we ourselves may have the background and experience with a particular culture to judge the merits of a film, but as multicultural educators, we are often in the position of dealing with cultures not in our area of expertise. What steps can we take to ensure the validity and integrity of our materials?

This concern applies not only to documentaries but also to feature films. While documentaries are held to a standard of truth and accuracy different from fictional productions, feature films must be scrutinized as well for the ways in which they depict cultures. Does the film demonstrate knowledge of and respect for a culture, or is its treatment careless and shallow? Even though plot and characterization may be fictional, feature films, like literary fiction, can reveal profound truths about people and cultures, or they can distort and misrepresent.

A central question in using multicultural films has to do with the background and credentials of the director. Is the director a member of the culture depicted or an outsider? This question of insider and outsider cannot be ignored in interpreting multicultural films; on the contrary, it serves as a valuable and necessary point of reference. (In chapter 7, four antiapartheid films are discussed in terms of who made them. In chapter 8, the same questions are posed with respect to films about Native Americans.)

At the same time, information on the director's personal background alone serves neither to validate nor invalidate the film. It is well known that outsiders can prove keen observers of other cultures, noticing traits virtually invisible on the inside. Nor does being an insider in itself guarantee depth of perception or insight. Nonetheless, films do not exist in a vacuum, and information about the director's personal background and experiences aids not only in establishing credibility, but in understanding and interpreting the film.

An interesting case in point is the production of Alice Walker's Pulitzer prize-winning novel *The Color Purple* by director Steven Spielberg. The enormous controversy unleashed by this film had nothing to do with Spielberg's qualifications as a filmmaker per se, but rather with his qualifications to direct this particular film. As critic Kathi Maio explains succinctly, "The failures of the movie are directly linked to Spielberg's limitations as a *white man* glibly attempting to tell the story of a *black woman*."[4] In her review of the film, Maio argues that Spielberg and Dutch-born Menno Meyjes, who wrote the screenplay, "alter Walker's story at will, to their own white, male, politically astute sensibilities."[5]

Other critics have been equally vociferous in their criticism of the film. Black feminist writer Michele Wallace called it the "Amos 'n' Andy of the 80s," and many critics railed against its depiction of African-American males, calling it, for example, a "hate letter to black men."[6] But the worst offense is undoubtedly, as Donald Bogle claims, the film's "failure to give the viewer the very thing that made the novel so powerful," namely, the voice of its main character Celie. Spielberg lost what Walker had accomplished— the creation of a black woman character "American fiction had long ignored or overlooked."[7]

The case of *The Color Purple* is instructive because it shows how complex the issue becomes when original author, screenwriter, and director—from three different backgrounds—collaborate to shape a new work. Also, it shows how far critical and public opinion can diverge on multicultural issues. Many critics disliked the film, and the NAACP and other African-American groups protested, but, as Bogle points out, many other critics praised the film, and "millions of moviegoers, many of whom were black, *loved* it, seeing the picture as the first full-scale screen examination of the experiences and tensions of black women."[8]

For the purposes of cross-cultural learning, it is important above all to be informed about the director (and occasionally about the original author and screenwriter) and to be aware that questions surrounding who makes what films can be highly sensitive and controversial. Relevant background information is generally accessible for well-known authors and directors but can be quite scarce for independent and documentary filmmakers. Among the best reference works on the subject are *World Film Directors* (edited by John Wakeman) and the *International Directory of Films and Filmmakers* (edited by Nicolas Thomas). Film criticism, film histories, and screenplays or companion volumes to films all may provide valuable information. For example, a volume entitled *Dances with Wolves: The Illustrated Story of the Epic Film* provides commentaries by director/star Kevin Costner, producer Jim Wilson, and screenwriter Michael Blake. The book documents their extensive collaboration with Native-American consultants to achieve authenticity and describes the Native-American actors' views on their participation. Similarly, the book *Do the Right Thing*, which contains both Spike Lee's journal, written during the creation of the script, and his production notes, provides insights into Lee's role as an African-American director.

Related to the qualifications of the filmmaker is the question of advisers. Did the director work with experts and area specialists? Usually the names of advisers and specialists are listed in production credits. While it may be difficult to judge the qualifications of these specialists, one can at least check to see if experts were consulted.

Filmographies that are critically annotated by specialists serve as a further aid. One such work, Bill J. Gee's *Asian-American Media Reference Guide*, is an excellent resource, describing more than one thousand audiovisuals on Asian Americans available in the United States. Annotated filmographies on black films include *The Afro-American Cinematic Experience: An Annotated Bibliography and Filmography* by Marshall Hyatt and *Frame by Frame: A Black Filmography* by Phyllis Rauch Klotman. African-American Donald Bogle's *Blacks in American Films and Television* provides in-depth, informative film descriptions and critiques. Though not a filmography, Gary D. Keller's *Chicano Cinema* includes a number of important research articles and reviews.

You might also consult area specialists on your own for evaluations and recommendations. I often ask colleagues from relevant academic departments for assistance; while their opinions may vary, it is nonetheless important to know the thinking of specialists. I also ask nonspecialists—students, friends, and colleagues—to help me evaluate how their cultures are portrayed in films. Did they find any inaccuracies? Did anything offend them? What did they find particularly insightful or revealing? International students, in particular, can give valuable feedback about how their cultures are depicted.

Furthermore, evaluations from colleagues, friends, and students familiar with the particular culture can help you determine if the film is out-of-date. While some films, particularly those dealing with classical theater or dance, architecture, religious ritual, or historical topics may be useful for many years, films intended to depict contemporary issues can become rapidly outdated. This does not mean that they cannot be used, but the information and visuals must be supplemented by an update. While feature films do not become outdated in the same way as documentaries, for our purposes they also need to be placed unmistakably within a historical context.

Locating and Using Film Reviews

As you evaluate films, you will find that film reviews are an indispensable resource. Reviews, both from mainstream and alternative press sources, offer a wide range of helpful opinions, criticism, and information, but locating them can be a time-consuming process.

The most important reference work for reviews of films released in major markets in the United States is Jerome Ozer's *Film Review Annual*. For each film included, the *Annual* provides several important reviews, in their entirety, from major periodicals and newspapers. It also provides references for locating additional reviews. To give an example, the 1984 volume includes eight full-length reviews of *The Ballad of Gregorio Cortez* (page 83) from sources such as *Cineaste*, the *Los Angeles Times*, and the *Village Voice*. Readers are also referred to additional reviews in the *New York Times* and *Variety*. The *Film Review Annual* has appeared yearly since 1982, and each volume contains reviews of hundreds of films. The *Annual* is a marvelous resource, very pleasurable to use, and it basically does much of our work for us.

Other important reference works are the *New York Times Film Reviews* and *Variety's Film Reviews*, yearly compilations of these publications' own film critiques, arranged chronologically and indexed by title. *Magill's Cinema Annual*, published yearly since 1982 as a supplement to the twenty-one-volume core set entitled *Magill's Survey of Cinema*, contains one in-depth review for each film as well as references to sources of additional reviews. The 1991 volume reviews ninety-four significant films released in the United States the previous year.

For reviews of films produced worldwide, the most important reference work is Nicolas Thomas's *International Directory of Films and Filmmakers*. It is up-to-date (the second edition was published in 1990) and contains two volumes: *Films* and *Directors/Filmmakers*. For each entry, it provides full credits for the film, followed by a comprehensive bibliography of books, articles, and reviews as well as an essay by a film specialist. The *International Dictionary of Films and Filmmakers* (edited by Christopher Lyon), follows a similar format, providing credits, a bibliography, and a review. A second edition appeared in 1990 in two volumes: one for films and one for directors.

The *Reader's Guide to Periodical Literature* also provides easily accessible, up-to-date information on sources of film reviews. Films are listed by individual title under the heading "Motion Picture Reviews—Single Works."

If you have access to on-line technology, you may be able to retrieve references to film reviews, usually by searching under the film title. Depending on the databases to which you have access, however, on-line searches can be expensive and cumbersome.

While the reference tools discussed above are enormously helpful, they have limitations. First, they are geared primarily to feature films rather than documentaries. Sources you might check for documentary reviews include *Video Librarian, Booklist, Landers, Sightlines,* and *Librarian's Video Review*. The *Media Review Digest* is a comprehensive annual index of reviews of nonprint media appearing in numerous periodicals and other sources.

Furthermore, many of the above reference tools are geared to the mainstream media. Clearly, it is important to know how major newspapers, periodicals, and film journals respond to films, but to gain a more complete and balanced picture, we also need to investigate reactions in the alternative press as well as in ethnic and minority publications. With few exceptions, these less widely circulated publications are generally not indexed anywhere. You might begin by familiarizing yourself with a few nonmainstream media publications as sources of film reviews. If, for example, you are showing *Zoot Suit* (page 147), you can check the Hispanic press. If you are showing *Winds of Change* (page 124), you can try to locate Native-American newspapers such as the *Lakota Times*. Though outdated, the *Encyclopedic Directory of Ethnic Newspapers and Periodicals* might be useful in providing ideas and direction.

Aesthetic Criteria

Although we are not primarily involved with film aesthetics, artistic merit is of more than just passing interest in selecting cross-cultural materials. A compelling script, fine acting, and beautiful photography will not guarantee cross-cultural validity, but the viewer is much more likely to be captured by an excellent film than by a poor one. If the visual images, for example, of a stunningly photographed film like Godfrey Reggio's *Koyaanisqatsi* (page 79) remain with the viewer long after its showing, then Reggio's notion of modern technological "culture" as a world out of balance—as contrasted with the natural landscapes revered by the Hopi—will have been conveyed with special force. And if the performances of Sissy Spacek and Whoopi Goldberg in *The Long Walk Home* (page 91) are convincing, viewers will undoubtedly be more receptive to the film's cross-cultural themes.

There are so many magnificent feature films with cross-cultural themes currently available that it hardly seems defensible to choose a second-rate production, unless it is chosen with a special purpose in mind (see chapter 5 for a discussion of this point). Nor does a documentary have to be dry and pedantic; films such as *American Tongues* (page 54) are highly creative and entertaining, and those such as *Racism 101* (page 115) and *A Class Divided* (page 50) are so powerful as to hold most viewers spellbound.

Because of my predisposition toward well-crafted productions, I am generally not inclined to favor didactic films made specifically to enhance cross-cultural understanding. These easily end up being of the talking-head variety, heavy on morals and lessons, but punchless and flat in terms of interest. Nonetheless, they should not be dismissed entirely, and some of the most effective ones will be included. All feature films and documentaries discussed in the following chapters have been chosen with artistic standards in mind and can, in my judgment, be considered fine films independent of their cross-cultural content.

As a final word here, one does not have to be a film critic in order to develop confidence in a self-styled set of aesthetic expectations. Most of us have grown up with television and film, and we can probably do quite well by applying our homegrown standards, while turning to film reviews for assistance.

The Harshest Critics

The more we use films, the more we learn about their power and effectiveness from our own students. The students' reactions are invaluable in helping us to judge films and improve our pedagogy. Students tend to be harsh critics, since they easily become bored or inattentive. Any film must pass the first test of holding student interest if it is to remain on the active list. At the same time, reactions vary from group to group and from year to year; some films may be flops with certain groups and hits with others.

While students may not like some films, that in itself is not necessarily a signal for rejection. I was very pleased, for example, when a student recently wrote an angry essay, entitled "That Awful Film," about *Managing the Overseas Assignment* (page 153). The student was offended at how Americans were stereotyped as stupid, insensitive clods in the five dramatic scenes. Personally, I like the film, precisely because insightful students tend to rebel against its treatment of Americans. They then begin to see the insidiousness of stereotyping and to question the appropriateness of using stereotypes, even in this context.

3

How to Use Cross-Cultural Films:
Thoughts on Pedagogy

I do not think that using a book is the best way to learn teaching methods, nor do methods and techniques that work for one person necessarily work for another. At the same time, it seems unnecessary for each teacher to reinvent the wheel. Often new ideas can serve as stimuli, can be transformed to suit one's own purposes, experiences, and personality. Ideas and suggestions in this book are meant as starting points. They come from my own experiences in teaching classes on intercultural communication and preparing undergraduates for study abroad, as well as from my participation in a variety of cross-cultural courses and workshops.

The basic premise for the pedagogy described in this book is that cross-cultural films should not stand alone—as an add-on, filler, or afterthought—but rather should be firmly embedded in an instructional unit. In most cases, this unit should include both warm-up and follow-up components.

Warming Up

Because of time limitations, we are often tempted to show films with little or no group preparation; if the film runs an hour, we can hardly even find a few minutes at the end of a session for follow-up discussion, much less for activities beforehand. Yet warm-up is often critical to the success of a film showing. Whether the students are receptive—whether they are distracted by extraneous elements or attuned to the essence of a film—may hinge on as little as a few sentences of introduction.

Some of my own greatest disappointments in using film have resulted, I am now convinced, from my failure to lay the ground-

25

work for the film. In one case, I was particularly excited about a wonderful Cable News Network documentary entitled *Global Report 1985*, which I thought would be perfect preparation for an orientation session of seventy-five undergraduates planning for a semester abroad. But the students seemed bored and inattentive during the showing, and the irrefutable evidence of this came in their evaluations of the orientation. One student, in a typical comment, wrote that the film was a waste of time, since what she needed was "practical information" about going to Vienna, not "a lecture about the Third World."

I realized that I had failed to set the stage for the film, falsely assuming that the topic itself would capture the students' interest. In a brief introduction, perhaps I could have asked the students what types of global issues they were thinking about—regardless of whether their particular destination was Europe, Asia, or Latin America—as they prepared to venture out into the world themselves. Or I could have asked them how a familiarity with international issues might benefit them during their international travel and study. In any case, I needed to explain that there would be a barrage of country-specific information later in the orientation. Confused as to why we were not dealing with their particular destinations, most of the students viewed the film with impatience and irritation.

I made a similar mistake when showing two films from the *Going International* series—*Bridging the Culture Gap* (page 152) and *Managing the Overseas Assignment* (page 153)—to another group of college undergraduates preparing to go abroad. After the first unsuccessful showings, I discovered that the students found the films unsuitable, since they were made for business executives. Now I simply tell the group prior to viewing that, while the films were made for business executives, similar principles apply to educational travel, so they should not be distracted by the references to business. This simple caveat seems to work; the students now do not appear the least bothered by the business context, but even seem to enjoy comparing their own world of education to the business environment presented in the films.

If you are using a foreign film—particularly from the Third World (see page 106 for a discussion of this terminology)—the warm-up should include hints on how to view non-Hollywood productions. Accustomed to slick, fast-paced, high-budget productions, students may judge a film to be of poor quality—and even dismiss it altogether—simply because it does not meet their technological expectations. As Cornelius Moore points out in his pamphlet introducing viewers to African videos available through California Newsreel, one must try to view African films "through African eyes." To get the most out of films which are "often beautiful, sometimes humorous, and always engaging," he says, viewers must "look at them in a new way":

> Many African films deliberately explore a different style from European and Hollywood films. Scenes unfold at a measured pace, with the deliberation of story-telling or fairy tales. Shots are often framed to reveal the larger social patterns of rural life. The acting sometimes seems a little formal, almost reticent. Don't fight these differences; try to appreciate the timeless rhythms and ordered life of a less industrialized society.[1]

If the film presupposes certain historical knowledge, as is often the case with international films, it is important to provide background information beforehand. *The Go Masters* (page 112), for example, can hardly be understood without rudimentary knowledge of Sino-Japanese conflicts in this century. While the information does not have to be greatly detailed, a brief historical review, accompanied by a handout outlining the most important dates and events—especially those which figure in the plot, such as the Nanjing massacre of 1937—will help to avoid needless confusion and make the film more meaningful.

In an ESL class, warm-ups for films should also include information necessary for comprehension, such as explanations of key vocabulary and concepts as well as names and places. As an example, in preparation for the video series *Eyes on the Prize* (page 144), you might review terms such as "segregation," "integration," and "boycott"; people such as Rosa Parks, Martin Luther King, Jr., and Malcolm X; organizations such as NAACP, SNCC, and SCLC; and places such as Montgomery and Selma. The same type of preparation is important in foreign-language classrooms, especially if films are to be shown without subtitles.

A warm-up, particularly if it requires the students to do some type of preparation, also serves to heighten anticipation and curiosity. If the students know something about the film and have a personal investment in seeing it as a result of reading or other preparations, the learning will likely be more intense than if they are hit with it cold. Thus it is advisable to begin laying the groundwork early, letting students know, for example, that "this topic will be explored in greater depth when we see the film *The Color of Honor*" (page 122). You should also be sure to include at least the titles of films in syllabi and in workshop descriptions.

As part of the preparation for film viewing, facilitators may wish to introduce some general information about the medium itself. While it is certainly not necesary to offer detailed explanations of film language and techniques (nor would most of us have the expertise to do so), it is nonetheless important to help students become aware of some basics. Depending on the extent to which you intend to use film with a particular group, you might assign some readings on film and discuss guidelines for viewing. The following quotation from *The American Indian in Film*, by Michael Hilger, illustrates how knowledge of film techniques can illuminate viewing:

> The long shot, which emphasizes the setting, often stresses the landscape of the West, with either hostile Indians hiding and threatening to attack or conquered Indians vanishing into the horizon in long processions. High-angle shots, in which the audience looks down on the subject, may suggest the vulnerability of the whites about to be ambushed by Indians. Low-angle shots...

can emphasize the threat of the Indian lurking
above his victims.[2]

Hilger further explains how editing, especially crosscutting
between pursuers and pursued, increases fear of the threatening
Indians, and composition, which places white heroes in higher or
more central positions in the picture, reinforces the idea that
Indians are inferior. Music, in the form of hostile drums and
rescuing bugle calls, and acting roles that reduce the Indian either
to wooden masks that barely speak or else to fierce, war-whooping
warriors also send clear messages to the audience.

In addition to covering some of these basics of film, you might
wish to discuss with students the idea of truth as reflected on the
screen, especially when showing documentaries. Students should
understand that while documentaries are indeed meant to tell
"real" or factual stories rather than fictional ones, the reality
presented is a constructed one, and the truth is one person's truth—
the filmmaker's. With a little practice, students can begin to see
how the documentary filmmaker's use of the medium—the selection of camera shots, sequencing of shots, choice of music, and
voice-over narrations—expresses a point of view. That it is a point
of view and not an objective truth is a critical distinction.

Clearly, if you are using a film in a two-hour workshop, the
warm-up will have to be brief and will likely occur immediately
prior to viewing. If, however, you are teaching a class over a period
of weeks or months, then the warm-up can be more extensive and
need not take place on the same day as the showing. You may well
wish to assign certain readings before the viewing. Examples of
warm-up readings will be given as individual films are discussed in
subsequent chapters.

As useful and important as warm-ups can be, they become
counterproductive if overdone. In particular, information which
destroys suspense or drama will diminish the enjoyment and effect
of a film. Nor does it seem advisable to use study guides which
predispose students to watch the film in a certain way. If students

are admonished to watch for or keep track of certain things, their own spontaneous reactions to the film may be lost.

Viewing the Film

A number of important questions arise about the best way to view a film. Is it necessary for the group to view the film together in the classroom, or can students be assigned to watch a video outside class? Does the facilitator need to watch the film with the group? Should students who have already seen the film sit through it again? Should the facilitator interrupt the film to make certain points, or should the integrity of the film as a whole be upheld?

If at all possible, intercultural films should be viewed *as a group* with the facilitator present. While you may feel a strong temptation to save class time by sending students on their own to the media center, you should resist except in rare cases. What is lost in order to save time is quite simply the most valuable part—the group experience.

The experience of watching a cross-cultural film with other people is very different from watching it alone. As a member of an audience, one is aware of—and affected by—the reactions of others. Whether there is laughter or tears, yawning, idle chatter or hushed silence, the viewer is part of a communal response. If emotions are running high, the group can form a bond—almost as if they have been through an intense experience together. This can be an invaluable aid to discussion afterwards—the shared emotion during the film carries over into the discussion.

The more the group is mixed by ethnicity, race, or nationality, the more stimulating and complex becomes the viewing. As students wonder how particular people are reacting to the film, they are learning one of the most important intercultural skills—how to see events from the other's point of view. The presence of several Japanese Americans, for example, in a viewing of *Come See the Paradise* (page 144), which tells of the internment of a Japanese-American family during World War II, will undoubtedly affect the way that others react to the film. Embarrassment, worry, guilt, and discomfort might emerge as one thinks of how the Japanese Americans are responding. In any case, a white or Hispanic American cannot watch the film in quite as cool or dispassionate a fashion when sitting next to a Japanese American.

In multicultural audiences, there are often noticeable differences in responses to humor. Viewers from one cultural or ethnic group may catch on to certain references or insinuations which are lost on outsiders without an intimate knowledge of that culture. In a showing of *Straight Out of Brooklyn* (page 136), for example, I noticed that African Americans sitting near me were laughing out loud at times when I had no idea why. My lack of comprehension came in part from simply not understanding some of the dialogue in Black English, but it is likely that even if I had heard the words, I might have missed the humor.

If films are subtitled, speakers of the original language may react differently from others, usually because they understand more than the subtitles communicate or because some subtitles are lacking, but sometimes because they find the translation to be wrong. Japanese students watching *Tokyo Pop* (page 163) in an ESL class, for example, will understand Japanese song lyrics as well as dialogue for which subtitles are occasionally not provided. In postfilm discussions, these students can act both as linguistic and cultural resources, translating certain segments and interpreting the events from the Japanese point of view.

Because a film will affect each group of viewers differently, the instructor must view the film along with class members to ascertain the group's unique response to it. Not only does the instructor need to be attuned to the group's reactions when facilitating follow-up discussion and activities, but being absent can give a message that the film is not very important.

Nor should students who have already seen a film be excused from another viewing. You might wish to explain that one often gets more out of a film the second time, that it is possible to focus more on details and subtleties, that it might be interesting to compare reactions the first time with present reactions. You might also mention that you yourself have seen the film numerous times and that each time you discover something new. If the film is a good one, it benefits from multiple viewings; moreover, students need to have the film fresh in their minds for follow-up activities.

One of the most important insights for cross-cultural educators in using film is to break with the idea that films need to be seen in their entirety. From the artistic point of view, it might well be that a film should be shown as a whole, without interruptions. But here we are *using* film as a tool for cross-cultural learning, not studying the art form. Because commercial films, especially, are not neat pedagogical units, we may need to cut, interrupt, and otherwise take liberties with film to achieve our purposes. Indeed, the most effective instruction might well be built around a five-minute segment of a full-length feature film. A good short segment can easily provide stimulation for a full hour of discussion.

Clearly, however, editing and interrupting have to be done with discretion. The students should not become irritated at constant interruptions, nor should they feel that they have unnecessarily been left hanging at particularly suspenseful parts. If only segments are shown, information can be provided on how to obtain the film for viewing in its entirety.

A final word about the physical set-up of the viewing room. As cross-cultural educators, most of us are well aware of the importance of space. Before showing the film, you should ask students to arrange their chairs so that they can all see and hear comfortably. Ideally, chairs should be arranged in a semicircle to avoid having to move them again for the discussion.

Following Up

What happens when the lights go on? Even if the time is very short, it is almost always better to allow for some group discussion immediately following the film. If the film has been long, one might wish to take a short break, but the group should then come back together to debrief. Only if there is no time to continue should discussion be postponed to a later date. By the time the group meets again, the strongest reactions will probably be gone, and students may have forgotten important details. Also, if students are upset or distressed, they need an opportunity to express themselves—and to hear others—on the spot.

The importance of allowing for immediate discussion was brought home to me when I scheduled an afternoon viewing of *El Norte* (page 72) for my class in the media center. I made the mistake of not being present myself, thinking that we could simply discuss the film in the next class session. To my surprise, a number of students came looking for me in my office after the film. They admitted to being very upset (one said she had cried throughout the film), and clearly they felt a need to talk right away, not at the next class meeting.

In facilitating film discussions, one should allow students first to express their feelings and emotions rather than move immediately into abstractions and theoretical debate. If students feel they are expected to "say something intelligent" as their initial reaction, they will probably not reveal anything personal. It is, however, their personal reactions which, at least at the outset, are the most important and need to be recognized.

An excellent technique for facilitating discussion along these lines is the "image-sound skim," described by Richard A. Lacey in his book *Seeing with Feeling: Film in the Classroom*. Lacey disagrees with the commonly held view "that 'I saw' is less important than 'I think.'"[3] Rather than forcing students to play "Deep Inner Meanings,"[4] a game in which they produce what they think the teacher wants to hear, the image-sound skim gives "everybody a chance to talk without fear of being wrong" and encourages students "to think in terms of the film itself."[5]

To conduct the image-sound skim, the facilitator asks students to mention visual images or sounds from the film that immediately come to mind. These serve as excellent springboards for discussion, and the "art of the film, instead of being killed by excessive analysis, has a fair chance to continue working on the audience." Lacey explains that "rhythms, details of setting, mood, counterpoints, transitions, color, and lighting subtly affect the processes by which students recall images and sounds."[6] An image-sound skim for *Do the Right Thing* is provided in chapter 8 (page 133).

In addition to the image-sound skim, there are other ways to avoid the tendency to begin immediate intellectualizing. You might simply ask the class to take a few minutes to jot down personal reactions to the film: What surprised? Upset? Bothered? Pleased? Discouraged you? Then you can begin the discussion by asking for some of these reactions. Students may be more willing to reveal personal responses if they have first had a chance to think and make a few notes. This approach also helps to bridge the sometimes uncomfortable gap between the film's conclusion and the beginning of discussion.

Depending on time available, one of the most valuable techniques you can use in the course of discussion is to view at least parts of films again. As with literature, one is a naive viewer the first time through, absorbed in the narrative flow and enjoying the elements of suspense. It is the second or third exposure that allows for more detailed and critical analysis. A second viewing often reveals totally new insights and allows for a much more sophisticated interpretation.

Role of the Facilitator

Regardless of how one chooses to proceed with discussion, the role of facilitator is critical. The challenges are enormous, and one learns something new from every film discussion.

As cross-cultural facilitators, we might best think of our role in terms of conducting a seminar or workshop rather than teaching a class. Facilitators will be more successful if they avoid slipping into the traditional student-teacher role, which assumes that the teacher is the expert, in possession of the right answers and poised to judge. In cross-cultural discussions, we are all learning from each other.

In stepping down from a lofty, protected position, the facilitator gives up a great deal of power and status, but this willingness to join in as a learner can make all the difference. I have come to believe that one of the most important things I can do as a facilitator is to show that I do not have all the answers, but am struggling with the issues myself. After years of thinking that I had to be objective and unemotional in the classroom, I now allow myself to reveal personal concerns, worries, and doubts.

At the same time, I do not think it appropriate for the facilitator to talk too much or become the main focus of attention. The most successful and exhilarating discussions, I find, are the ones in which students begin to talk among themselves, almost forgetting that I am there. The same is true from my experiences as a participant in cross-cultural workshops and seminars. What I remember best—and what meant the most to me—was what I learned from the other participants. Their reactions to films, particularly if they were very different from my own, remain vivid in my mind.

One of the most difficult challenges for the facilitator is to strike a balance between setting a specific agenda—which is almost guaranteed to stifle discussion—and allowing the discussion to become a free-for-all. How does one maintain direction and purpose, but allow for spontaneity? How does one know when digressions are useful, as opposed to taking the discussion too far off track? While there are no definite answers to these questions, the facilitator does need to avoid being controlling. What one intends to accomplish as facilitator is not likely to be useful if it is imposed on the group. At the same time, the discussion can fall apart if the facilitator does not provide direction when needed.

Facilitators must also be prepared to work in what is currently a highly charged atmosphere. Controversies over political correctness and the limits of free speech in the academy place us in a paradoxical position. Clearly, we do not wish to cause offense, but sometimes offensive or hurtful things are said, usually inadvertently, as students grapple with complex, emotional issues. We need to be ready to defend free speech, insofar as students must be allowed to express fears, ignorance, and prejudice in an educational process. Of ultimate importance is not so much what is said but the *context*. If a confused student admits in a classroom to feelings of prejudice against a certain ethnic group, that is quite different from yelling a racial epithet on the street at a stranger from that ethnic group. Perhaps this distinction seems obvious, but as debates over politically correct speech continue, we need to keep in mind that while the academy has the obligation to protect its members, it also must allow them to admit their shortcomings, to make mistakes and learn from them.

Because the field of intercultural communication is relatively new, because it is interdisciplinary, and because its material is often so sensitive, many educators find themselves in need of additional study and training. A French professor, for example, even with an extensive background in French language, literature, and culture, may wish to learn more of the theory and practice of intercultural communication to deal more knowledgeably with French-American interactions. For those seeking additional background and experience, conferences and workshops sponsored by professional associations such as NAFSA: Association of International Educators and SIETAR International (Society for Intercultural Education, Training, and Research) are a good place to start. The Institute of Culture and Communication at the East-West Center in Hawaii sponsors summer workshops for college and university faculty, and every summer the Intercultural Communication Institute in Oregon also offers a wide range of outstanding week-long courses on relevant topics.[7]

A final word about facilitation has to do with emotions in the classroom. As multicultural educators, we need to expect that the films we use and the ensuing discussions may provoke intense emotion and, at times, tears. The first time a student cried in my class, I was not only upset myself, but at a loss about what to do or say; now I know that dampness is part of the process and not to be avoided. On the contrary, allowing for personal reactions and feelings can help students begin to learn in new, more profound ways.

As you gain experience with expressions of emotion in the classroom and react more comfortably yourself, they will seem more natural and acceptable to everyone. You may well find that other class members handle the situation quite well, offering a touch on the shoulder from a neighboring seat or approaching the person afterwards for a private talk. Depending on the situation, you might offer a tissue and ask the person if she or he wishes to talk about what was upsetting or prefers simply to take a breather.

Keeping a Journal

Since not everyone is comfortable or proficient when speaking in groups, it is a good idea to provide for other avenues of expression. Because the journal gives students opportunities to reflect on what they have seen or heard and to define their own views, it is an excellent vehicle for this expression.

Despite the more widespread use and growing currency of the journal as a pedagogical tool, many students are still unfamiliar with it. They either confuse it with a diary, and thus include all types of extraneous information, or they revert to their more familiar term-paper format. Should you decide to use a journal, you might wish to provide guidelines in order to avoid such confusion and misunderstanding.

The basic idea behind journal entries is that they allow students to express personal reactions and to record impressions of the moment that otherwise are lost. If you are teaching a class, journals with as many as twenty or thirty entries over the period of several months can help students trace their own process of thinking and learning. Even in a shorter seminar or workshop, you might take five or ten minutes at appropriate times to ask students to record their thoughts and impressions. This type of exercise, even if very brief, helps students examine their views and focus their thinking.

Although journals are often deeply personal, they should nonetheless be collected and carefully read. While feedback in the form of nonjudgmental comments is very important, assigning grades seems to me unethical and counterproductive; how could one presume to grade another person's private deliberations and reflections?

I like to read sections from journals aloud to the rest of the group, since all kinds of insights are revealed on paper which simply do not come out in discussion. Of course, the passages have to be carefully selected so as to respect the students' privacy. Even though I ask students to mark sections which they do not wish to be read aloud, before class I ask permission to read unmarked sections if they seem sensitive. I do not identify the writer, but certain clues often reveal the identity of the person, especially once students come to know one another. This has never been a problem; on the contrary, the students rather seem to enjoy the idea that they are becoming better known to each other. Since I usually read short excerpts, I tend to read them myself, but if the passage is a long one, or if the student has written a poem or short story, I might ask a willing student to read.

In addition to providing students ample opportunity to write freely about whatever is on their minds, I also like to make some specific journal assignments. In response to film, students seem to prosper with assignments that are imaginative and personal, rather than those that elicit specific answers. Many creative ideas for journal assignments can come as film spin-offs—inviting students to forge a personal connection with characters or to play the role of scriptwriter or director. Samples of questions one might ask include:

1. Which character in this film would you most like to talk to in person? What would you say to that individual? How do you think he or she would respond?

2. Which character in this film would you least like to meet or talk to? Why?

3. Imagine a conversation between character x and character y on the topic of z. How might the script for this scene look?

4. Describe how character x would respond to the idea that _____?

5. What was character x really thinking when _____?

These types of questions, varied and adapted to the film in question, can provide a valuable exercise, not only because they allow exploration of multiple perspectives but also because they help to reveal the often surprising complexity of the issues at hand.

Another type of productive response to films is the assignment intended for the world outside the classroom. For example, after viewing the documentary *River People: Behind the Case of David Sohappy* (page 73), students might write letters to Congress or to their college or local newspapers about the issue of fishing rights for Native Americans and for the 1993 Supreme Court decision on it. Or they might write a review of the film for a local paper. Regardless of whether these writings are ever actually sent to their intended destinations—a decision which should be left to the students—the assignments themselves serve to sharpen the students' positions and prepare for other real-life writing in the future.

Reading Assignments

Reading assignments can be useful both before and after viewing films. Ideally, the assignments will allow students to see the issues from multiple perspectives. If, for example, you are viewing *Winds of Change* (page 124), readings by contemporary Native-American authors such as Louise Erdrich, Michael Dorris, Paula Gunn Allen, or N. Scott Momaday would provide perspectives otherwise often neglected. Since Momaday narrates part of the film, it might be particularly interesting to read at least an excerpt from one of his works. You might also wish to assign selections from an anthology such as *The Portable North American Indian Reader*, edited by Frederick Turner.[8] In addition, students could do some detective work to locate copies of treaties and Supreme Court decisions referred to in the film.

Rapidly growing interest in multiculturalism across the country has resulted in a veritable boom in available literature, both fiction and nonfiction. Most larger bookstores carry a wide selection of titles, categorized under headings such as "Ethnic Studies" or "Multiculturalism," or simply under various ethnic groups. Excellent anthologies of multicultural readings are available,[9] and James Banks's *Teaching Strategies for Ethnic Studies* is an invaluable resource with extensive bibliographies provided for ten ethnic groups.[10]

You might also wish to assign readings on intercultural communication to help students gain an insight into the concepts and theories underlying the encounters they have witnessed on film.

For example, Robert Shuter's article, "The Hmong of Laos: Orality, Communication, and Acculturation,"[11] illuminates many of the problems experienced by oral peoples from Laos, as seen in films such as *Becoming American* (page 130).

Issues presented in films take on a new relevance when students see them reflected in current newspapers and magazines. Using the example of *Winds of Change*, you might ask students to trace certain issues having to do with Native Americans' sovereignty—whether in relation to fishing rights or gambling casinos—in the press. Besides the mainstream publications, students should try to find coverage in the alternative press to get a better idea of how Native Americans themselves view the issue.

In addition to making specific class assignments, you might suggest additional titles and sources for those who wish to pursue in greater depth the topics addressed in the film.

Role Plays

Role plays are an excellent way to help students see the other person's point of view and understand the complexity of cross-cultural issues. Because acting can make some people feel uncomfortable, role plays are most successful when done by volunteers; the others can observe and take part in the discussion afterwards.

The types of spin-off questions described on page 38 for writing assignments can also be the starting points for challenging role plays. They can be done with individuals playing different roles, or the class can be split into small groups, each charged with representing different characters or groups from the film. For example, after *Racism 101*, one group could be asked to play the role of BAM (Black Action Movement) members and one group, the university administration. Adding a third group of largely white faculty members or student government representatives might be interesting, even if they were not depicted in the film. In this particular case, the students should be given a clear task and allowed some time to prepare, but if the role play is less demanding, you might simply ask students to act it through on the spot.

In role plays, students learn from assuming roles close to their personal experiences as well as from more unfamiliar roles. For example, if Japanese take the part of American businessmen and Americans, of Japanese businessmen, this helps participants to empathize and keeps the role play from becoming too personal. Each side is forced to think about the other's motives, needs, and emotions. Allowing students to play themselves is useful as a means of exploring and testing their own views. In this type of role play, students are likely to reveal their prejudices and, with the proper guidance, can begin to confront them.

Field Work

The possibilities for field work as a follow-up to a film viewing are as numerous as they are exciting. Field work helps students understand how intercultural topics are relevant within their own lives and communities. They become more aware of the cultural diversity all around them and more conscious of their own role in cross-cultural interactions. They literally begin to see things which they had never noticed—how people interact, how they are treated, how they themselves react.

Among the many types of field work which you might consider are interviews, observations, investigative work, and site visits. For example, after viewing the film *Blue Collar and Buddha* (page 129), which deals with a Laotian community that has settled in Rockford, Illinois, you might ask students to 1) interview an immigrant from Indochina living in your community, 2) find out about Indochinese immigrants in your region—who they are, where they live, what their occupations are, etc., and 3) explore a neighborhood where Indochinese have settled. If first- or second-generation Indochinese immigrants are in the class, they can serve as valuable resource people.

Field work needs to be written up and, if possible, also presented to the group. Comparing field experiences with the film presentation can be extremely instructive. In the case of *Blue Collar and Buddha*, one might ask to what extent the students' own observations of a local Indochinese community agree with the film depiction of Rockford, Illinois.

Before and After

Because it is difficult—both for the facilitator and the students—to assess the effect of a film on attitudes and learning, some exercises might be done prior to viewing and then repeated afterwards. Students can be asked to compare the two samples of their work to see if they feel the film has influenced their thinking or attitudes.

Rather than asking specific questions, you might try the free-association method. Prior to showing a film on Native Americans, for example, ask students to take five minutes to write in their journals whatever comes to mind when they think of Native Americans. Unless they are Native American themselves, they may have trouble thinking of anything beyond the most stereotypical cultural fragments—tepee, Sacagawea, tomahawks. When the exercise is repeated after a film, their responses are usually much more sophisticated and thoughtful, and they may be shocked to see how limited their prefilm associations were.

Many students, if asked to write down what comes to mind in association with Indochinese refugees before seeing a film such as *Becoming American* or *Blue Collar and Buddha*, may not be able to write anything at all. Subsequently, they will see for themselves the marked difference one film can make in at least their awareness of a significant segment of life in the United States.

4

A *Chairy Tale* and Other Classics

The films discussed in this chapter are among the finest available for introducing cross-cultural issues. They can be used with any group, whether international students, businesspeople, or police officers. While some films become dated quickly, these classics are likely to be useful for years to come.

A Chairy Tale

A film long recognized as highly original and stimulating is the ten-minute A *Chairy Tale*. Produced by Norman McLaren in 1957, this parody on a fairy tale is simply told in black and white and without words, but with the enchanting musical accompaniment of Indian musicians Ravi Shankar, Chatur Lal, and Modu Mullick.

The only characters are a man and a common wooden chair. Conflict begins immediately on the stark set as the man enters with his book and attempts to sit down on the chair to read, only to find that the chair pulls away from him. The ensuing struggle between man and chair leads them through a broad range of emotions, from frustration to violence to a near ending of the relationship, until a breakthrough results in a fairy-tale happy ending.

In the first section of the film, the man tries to get his way. He goes through various stages, at first showing surprise and fright that the chair is resistant, then displaying caution as he inspects and touches it in an attempt to figure out what is going on. In a series of different approaches, he eases himself toward it, stalks it, tries to grab it, and then chases it around the room. The chase accelerates, finally taking place in fast motion, with the man racing wildly around the room and eventually losing sight of the chair. This segment of the film ends in violence, as the man finally wrestles with the chair, becomes entangled in it, and is thrown off.

A second phase of the interaction begins as the tired man, alone on the set, decides he can do without the chair after all. He wipes his brow and the floor with his handkerchief, sits down on the floor, and starts to read. Slowly but surely, the chair begins to edge back into view. As the chair approaches, the man notices it but acts uninterested. The chair nudges him, but the man pushes it away. The chair falls to the floor in a gesture of hurt, then approaches again and is kicked away. The man shakes his finger at the chair in disapproval, then gestures to it to come closer, strokes it gently, and attempts to sit. But the chair refuses to cooperate.

The critical phase of the film brings resolution. At a virtual dead end, the man begins to think for the first time—he begins to think *about the chair*. What might be its problem? What does it want? What is he doing wrong? He begins anew, trying to please, entertain, or otherwise win over the chair. He tickles it, rocks it like a baby, plays hopscotch, does a military march, dances the tango beside it and then with it. He dances around the room. Nothing is successful in soliciting cooperation, but the chair seems willing to be patient, even to the point of encouraging the man not to give up. The man thinks again. Finally, he puts his arms forward and bends down, acting like a chair. The chair leaps in the air for joy. The man dusts himself off with his handkerchief, and the chair leaps in the air again. Now the chair approaches and sits on the man for a few seconds, then jumps back off. The man approaches the chair, the two bow to each other, and the chair moves forward so the man can sit. The final caption reads, "And they sat happily ever after."

The film raises a variety of questions about empathy, exploitation, and communication. Those who see it for the first time are usually fascinated by the rapprochement and are eager to examine its stages. The action is fast-paced, and it is not always easy for viewers to recall the exact details, but it is clear that the man and chair have gone through no small effort to establish a new type of relationship. When they sit down together at the end, it is a different man and a different chair. Just what has transpired and how they communicated with each other make for stimulating discussion.

What makes the film especially intriguing within the cross-cultural context is the absence of words. All communication takes place in other ways. The film's attention to small details in conveying subtleties of nonverbal communication is remarkable. For example, when the man attempts to sit on the chair in the very beginning, he is so absorbed in his book that he does not even look at the chair, just pulls out his handkerchief and wipes off the seat and back. By contrast, at the end he looks straight at the chair and bows before sitting, this time sensitive enough to consider that his handkerchief might offend the chair. The man's facial expressions and body language throughout reveal his changing attitudes and feelings. Even the chair takes on a personality with body language and expressions of its own.

Another reason the film is an excellent way to begin an exploration of cross-cultural issues is that it addresses the topic of power directly. How does power influence, distort, damage communication across cultures? Can honest communication take place between people or groups if there is an inequality of power? Can a dependent or subservient person ever really feel free to communicate openly with the more powerful? Can those in power ever really listen to or respect the point of view of those perceived as having less power? While these questions, it would seem, rightfully belong at the heart of cross-cultural studies, they are often neglected or forgotten. Perhaps there is an assumption that power issues can temporarily be set aside in an isolated exchange of words or ideas. Perhaps the field of cross-cultural communication has been developed and defined by those who have traditionally been holders of power and thus may not be fully aware of its implications.

Whatever the case may be, in A *Chairy Tale*, the choice of man and chair places power at the center. Is it not the natural function of a chair to be sat upon? Is it not the human who is rightfully in control, who should have all the decision-making power, who should use the chair as he wishes? By giving the chair its own will, the film challenges basic assumptions about how we relate to others. If we imagine ourselves in any given interaction as the man, the one with more power, how does that affect the way we communicate? If we imagine ourselves as the chair, the one with less power, how does that affect the way we communicate?

The man-chair relationship proves to be a marvelous metaphor for cross-cultural relationships. In an introductory course on cross-cultural communication, I showed the film in the first class session and asked the students to write essays telling what the man-chair struggle reminded them of in their own lives. One student wrote an essay entitled "A Married Tale," in which a young, unappreciated wife finally asserts herself. Several other student essays also focused on men and women, while some revolved around parent-child or sibling relationships. Interestingly, it was not necessarily the parent or older sibling who was seen as occupying the more powerful man role. One student wrote about children who take their parents for granted and come to expect all sorts of privileges. Others also described manipulative young children who are determined to have their way. In a completely different vein, one student chose the relationship between a trainer and an animal: "A trainer cannot take for granted that an animal will automatically obey him and do tricks," but each "must develop a level of trust and respect" for the other. Several students depicted the United States as the man and a Third World country as the chair. Finally, one insightful student described the relationship between humans and the earth as resembling that between man and chair.

The power of this film in creating a metaphor was demonstrated many times throughout the course, as students asked themselves if certain attitudes or behaviors were like the man or like the chair. The idea of a simple chair rebelling against insensitive treatment and insisting on respect, such that in the end *both* man and chair are transformed, is one which captures the imagination.

A final note: in discussing the film, we are inclined to concentrate primarily on the perspective of the man—his feelings, his actions, and his development. Even my plot review above focuses primarily on the man. It could be an interesting exercise simply to ask students to describe the plot of the film from the point of view of the chair. The summary might begin like this:

> A man approaches me while intently absorbed in
> his book. He does not acknowledge my presence,
> except to wipe me off with his handkerchief, as if
> I were dirty. Continuing to ignore me, he turns
> his back and attempts to sit down. Of course, I am
> insulted and pull away. He seems a bit puzzled
> and begins to look me over.

Students will probably have difficulty remembering enough to describe the film accurately from the chair's perspective, and they may ask to see it again. This should be welcomed, since a second viewing *from a different perspective* is excellent practice in developing empathy.

Two Global Views

While A *Chairy Tale* presents the small world of an interaction between two parties, two films that take a global approach to relationships are One and No Frames, No Boundaries. They are both based on the changes in human consciousness brought about by twentieth-century space exploration. By suggesting that the planet as a whole should be our frame of reference, they provide a philosophical and ethical context for communication and cooperation across all artificial boundaries.

The organization Foundation for Global Community (formerly called Beyond War), which produced the film One in 1989, calls it "ten minutes of music, images, and a few brief words, designed to inspire in each one of us a profound sense of interdependence and interconnectedness of all life." It begins with the printed definition of "one": "existing, acting, or considered as a single unity, entity, or individual," followed by a view of earth from outer space. Several minutes of visual images with melodic background music show the diversity and beauty of the natural world. Whales and small fish, birds, a lion with its cub, and insects carrying leaves are a few of the living creatures depicted in natural settings. Landscapes of a coastline, a redwood forest, and snow-capped mountains help to create a harmonious mood. The next sequence of visuals, accompanied by harsher music, shows the threatened environment—oil slicks, garbage dumps, polluted beaches and air—as well as the social and political problems of overcrowding, hunger and poverty, crime, and finally civil unrest and war.

Tips for Use: *One*

Before viewing, have students individually or in small groups draw a map of the world. After viewing, ask them if they need to make changes or modifications. Discuss the maps and how their mental image of the world may have been affected by the film. You might wish to show and discuss thought-provoking maps such as the Turnabout Map, which depicts the Americas upside down (Laguna Sales, Inc., 7040 Via Valverde, San Jose, CA 95135), the Peters Projection, which depicts all world areas according to their actual size (Friendship Press, PO Box 37844, Cincinnati, OH 45222), and the *New Yorker* cover illustration of the world as seen from Ninth Avenue.

Can you remember times when you felt at one with your environment? With other people? With the world as a whole? Describe the feelings and what you think may have caused them.

Further Reading

Deep Ecology, Bill Devall and George Sessions (Salt Lake City: Gibbs M. Smith, 1985).
The Turning Point: Science, Society, and the Rising Culture, Fritjof Capra (Toronto: Bantam, 1982).

In the brief commentaries that follow, the worldview of oneness is discussed and given contours. Bill Moyers talks about how viewing the earth from above makes us aware that all of us are "in the same boat," a tiny, vulnerable, and "very crowded little vessel that we are sailing through space." James Joseph speaks of the concept of neighbor, suggesting that we are now in a process of "redefining who the neighbor is"; we need to transform our "commitment to the near neighbor to a commitment to the distant neighbor." And Joseph Campbell says that the "only myth that is going to be worth thinking about in the immediate future is one that's talking about the planet—not this city, not these people, but the planet and everybody on it." The film concludes with upbeat music and photographic images of people from many cultures around the world at work and play.

The idea that the world is one is also explored in *No Frames, No Boundaries*, which takes its title from reflections made by Apollo 9 astronaut Russell Schweikart as he traveled through space:

> When you go around the earth in an hour and a half, you begin to recognize that your identity is with that whole thing, and that makes a change....There are no frames. There are no boundaries.

I would not recommend using the entire film, since the first part tries to cover too much human history too quickly, but only the few minutes near the end, an unforgettable segment in which we experience the earth from outer space through Schweikart's words. As the viewers gaze at the distant planet, we hear his voice-over reflection that "on that small spot—that little blue and white thing—is everything that means anything to you. All of history and music and poetry and art and birth and love, tears, joys, games, all of it, on that little blue spot out there that you could cover with your thumb." He says that as you look down, you feel that "you know all those people down there, and they are like you, they are you....And somehow you recognize that you're a piece of this total life."

Both of these films are stimulating introductions to a new way of thinking. As Fred Hoyle predicted in 1948, "Once a photograph of the Earth, taken from the *outside*, is available...a new idea as powerful as any in history will be let loose."[1] While many of us may have heard phrases such as global consciousness or international perspective, almost to the point of becoming clichés, we may not have thought about how we personally are affected. The films give us the opportunity to ask fascinating questions about our own frames of reference: How do we feel about the idea that the world is one? Even if we find the idea appealing, are we really capable of seeing it as such? Where are our personal frames and boundaries? What criteria do we use for defining our own world? Whom do we consider a neighbor and why? What do we consider home and why? How might we broaden our concepts of neighbor and home?

As we examine these questions of oneness and separation, of unity and boundaries, we find ourselves at the heart of intercultural communication. Whom do we perceive as us, whom as them? What are the differences that divide us? Are there commonalities which might transcend these differences? How can we appreciate the differences?

Tips for Use: *No Frames, No Boundaries*

Before and after viewing, write down words you associate with the idea of "home." Did the film influence your concept of home?

What feelings do you have when looking at the picture of the "big blue spot" taken from outer space? Can you imagine what you might think and feel if you were able to view the earth from outer space?

Further Reading

The Home Planet, Kevin W. Kelley, ed. (Reading, MA: Addison-Wesley, 1988).

A Class Divided

As memorable and enlightening as cross-cultural films might be, there are few films which might be said to have the power to change lives. But if an individual film can possibly have such a profound effect as to change the way we think, then *A Class Divided*, produced in 1985 by Yale University Films as part of the PBS television news series *Frontline*, is one such film.

A *Class Divided* tells of a controversial experiment in discrimination performed over a period of years by third-grade teacher Jane Elliott in Riceville, Iowa. Elliott first tried the experiment in April 1968, as a means of responding to her pupils' distress over the assassination of Dr. Martin Luther King, Jr., who had been a class hero of the month. Elliott believed that her all-white, all-Christian class would have difficulty understanding what discrimination really means. She decided to have them *experience* discrimination by dividing the group according to eye color, with blue eyes being acknowledged as smarter, cleaner, and more civilized and receiving recess and lunchroom privileges. Browns had to wear collars so they could be easily identified, and they were not allowed to play with blues. The following day the roles were reversed.

The film focuses on one particular group of third graders who undergo the experiment in Elliott's class in 1970 and then participate in a class reunion with their former teacher fifteen years later. At the reunion, the adults reflect on the effect the experiment had on their lives and on their roles as parents. They all agree that the course of their lives was markedly changed by those two days in their elementary school classroom.

The documentary then shows how the eye-color experiment has been used as a teaching tool in education, government, business, and other organizations over the past fifteen years. For example, we learn that a film of the children undergoing the experiment is regularly shown to inmates in a maximum security prison as part of a sociology class. The inmates, almost exclusively black and Hispanic, clearly find the film relevant to their own lives and affirm its validity in combatting racism.

We also watch as Elliott uses the experiment in a different setting, giving a day-long workshop to a mostly white group of adult employees of the Iowa prison system, including prison guards and parole officers, as a means of sensitizing them to minority-inmates' concerns. She carries out the experiment, in which blue-eyed people are inferior, all morning in an atmosphere of tension and hostility. The afternoon debriefing yields astonishing results, as Elliott asks how it felt to be on one side or the other and probes into the reasons for the adults' passivity that morning. One white male with blue eyes who had been verbally attacked and denigrated by Elliott says he felt powerless and trapped, as if he were in a glass cage. He wanted to speak up to defend himself, but he thought that would only make the situation worse; he felt a sense of hopelessness. What amazed him is that he became so uncomfortable so quickly, within the first fifteen minutes. He said he realized during the morning session that there were very few times in his life he had ever felt discriminated against.

While the viewer may not feel the full impact of the lesson, as he or she might from actually participating in the experiment, the effect of the film is nonetheless powerful. The strongest reaction comes from watching the children, as they so quickly accept their teacher's absurd justification for judging each other. The rapid deterioration of friendships, the incidents of name-calling and fighting, and the demonstrable changes in perceptions of their intelligence and self-worth—all on the basis of eye color—leave the viewer dazed and disturbed. The degree of conformity is also distressing; though some of the children seem to know, or at least suspect, that the teacher is doing something wrong, no one knows how to stop her; it does not ever seem to occur to them to challenge her authority.

Shockingly, the same is almost as true of the adult prison employees, who, one might reasonably expect, should know better than to go along with such a ridiculous proposition. Some blues — who are being discriminated against—do, in fact, try to protest, but they do not gain the support of their own, nor do any browns come to their defense. No one refuses to continue; at one point, a blue-eyed woman threatens to leave, but decides otherwise.

At the end of the film, Elliott responds to a question about the desirability of wider use of the exercise by saying that the "necessity for this exercise is a crime." Rather than seeing it used more widely, she would like to see the necessity for it eliminated. But until the time that it is no longer needed, she is determined to try to inoculate her students against the "virus of bigotry."

College students who watched the film in my introductory intercultural communications courses were visibly moved, some to tears. Many felt upset and angry, some were disturbed and discouraged, others were sad. One student wrote that the film was overwhelming and that she went away from class "feeling very uptight about the situation." The mood afterwards was intense and sober; as one student wrote, "Today was a very heavy day. You could feel the heaviness at the end of the class."

Perhaps viewers react with such intensity and emotion because we, too, are being inoculated. Though not actually participating in the physical exercise ourselves, we nonetheless become part of it. As we see how easily both children and adults slip into discriminatory behavior, we are tempted to draw frightening conclusions about ourselves. At the same time, the film gives evidence that people can be jarred into facing their prejudices and reversing them, that people can actually *learn* not to be prejudiced.

This belief is at the core of cross-cultural education. However one might feel about the means used by Jane Elliott or however one might judge the results of her particular experiment, what she stands for is ultimately more important. She is taking the position that tolerance can be taught. Whether her means are justified and necessary, or perhaps too risky, can make for interesting class discussion. In my courses, some students recalled similar experiments done in their own classrooms, one in which roles were assigned as slaves and masters and one in which there were randomly selected in and out groups, with the out group having to wear yellow paper stars. In both cases, the students had mixed feelings about these experiences. In the latter case, the student remembered that the experiment got out of hand and had to be stopped. But she said the students had nonetheless learned something important about discrimination.

The ethical questions are complicated and far-reaching. Rather than avoiding them, however, this film encourages us to ask fundamental questions of ourselves and others about discrimination. As educators, we are challenged to venture into areas which we previously might have considered too controversial, too risky. Without glossing over or minimizing the problem, the film leaves us with the hope that, through education, a class divided might become a class united.

Tips for Use: *A Class Divided*

What do you think of the idea of "inoculating" people against prejudice? Can it work? What are the risks?

If you have ever been part of an experiment like the one described in the film, what happened? Was the experiment worthwhile for you? For the others?

If you had been a blue-eyed person in the prison employee workshop, how do you think you might have reacted? Or a brown-eyed person?

Plan to do a cross-cultural simulation such as BaFá BaFá (Simulation Training Systems, PO Box 910, Del Mar, CA 92014) or Barnga (Intercultural Press, PO Box 700, Yarmouth, ME 04096) with the class. Afterwards, have students reflect on their reactions to the simulation in light of the ideas presented in the film.

American Tongues

A fascinating look at attitudes Americans have about their speech is provided in *American Tongues*, an hour-long video which challenges commonly held biases toward certain accents or dialects. Beginning with the question, "Who do you think has a funny accent?" the film shows in lighthearted fashion how different people and groups all believe their own speech patterns to be normal. It's the others who have an accent; "They're the ones that are hard to understand." A man from the Appalachian area of Kentucky says candidly, "I thought this was the way everybody talked." A resident of Tangier Island, Virgina, says, in his especially distinct speech pattern: "I figure I sound just like Walter Cronkite." We are beginning to see that, in the film's own words, "Everybody speaks with an accent."

The film takes us to various parts of the country to illustrate that differences in speech relate to differences in how we lead our lives, how we deal with the world. As folklorist Cratis Williams says, speech is "culture expressing itself in sound." Norms of courtesy and respect in Appalachia, for example, mandate that one talk far around the subject before hitting it, whereas Texans find direct speech to be a sign of openness, honesty, and trustworthiness.

American Tongues does not shy away from the sensitive issue of which dialects are commonly considered to be more desirable and which less. We see the effect of stigmas attached to people with certain accents, as in the case of a woman from Brooklyn who reveals her embarrassment and distress at knowing that others look down on her because of her speech. As a sales representative, she is faced with the bias that "anyone who talks like that can't be very smart." A young Italian-American man from East Boston realizes that his speech is seen as uneducated but at the same time enjoys the fact that it gives him an image of sexual prowess.

Current controversy surrounding the use of Black English is also addressed. Educator Nona Stokes, who views Black English as a legitimate dialect that is "not bad English, not slang, not something that you have to look down upon," finds it difficult to reconcile her defense of Black English with her feeling that blacks still have to learn standard English. She concludes that language and politics cannot be separated. "I think that the majority of white America does not accept Black English," she says, "but not because of the language itself, [rather] because of the people who speak it."

Interviews with other African Americans reveal uncertainties and disagreements about their language. One man living in a white neighborhood admits that at times it grates on him when he hears his sons talk like white suburbanites. He asks himself, "My God...am I raising two white boys here?" In another scene, two men in a group gathered on the street disagree about the value of Black English. The first man is angry that his language is not respected: "You're made to believe that your own language, that you've been communicating with, is a bad language." The other man, however, discredits Black English: "When you're trying to increase your standard of living, believe me, black vernacular ain't going to mean no more than that cigarette butt lying on the ground."

As the narrator comments toward the end of the film, "Language can bring us together or set us apart." In its evenhanded, gentle approach, *American Tongues* helps to bring us together. By making speech differences seem enjoyable and intriguing, rather than merely odd or off-putting, and by explaining how some of the differences came to be and what they represent, the film helps us begin to accept and appreciate regionalisms which might otherwise tend to evoke mockery or derision. An especially nice touch is the Southern accent of the narrator, Polly Holliday, who serves as a persuasive example that voices in the media need not all be so uniform as we are led to believe.

Tips for Use: *American Tongues*

In small groups, try to identify your own accents and regionalisms. Does your description of your own accent fit with how others hear it? Have you ever felt discriminated against because of your speech?

Try to recall how you reacted to some of the accents you heard in the film. What judgments, if any, did you make about the people based on their speech?

Listen to yourself on a tape recorder and describe your impressions of your own speech.

Watch the Saturday morning cartoons to see how accents are used to create certain impressions.

Listen to the radio or television to see how many broadcasters or actors have detectable accents. Determine what responses these accents provoke for you.

Films Discussed

1. **American Tongues,** 1987, 56 mins., color, Center for New American Media.
2. **A Chairy Tale,** 1957, 10 mins., b/w, Int'l Film Bureau, Inc.
3. **A Class Divided,** 1985, 60 mins., color, PBS Video.

4. **No Frames, No Boundaries,** 1982, 21 mins, color, Foundation for Global Community (Palo Alto).
5. **One,** 1989, 10 mins., color, Foundation for Global Community (Palo Alto).

Related Films

1. **Balablok**
   1974, 8 mins., color, Encyclopedia Britannica Educational Corp. Animated film tells story of aggression between blocks of different shapes. Several cubes taunt a passing circle, resulting in an all-out war between the two sides. When the blocks are all sufficiently battered to resemble each other in hexagon shapes, peace seems likely, but then a triangle enters!

2. **Four Families**
   1959, 60 mins., b/w, CRM/McGraw Hill Films
   Anthropologist Margaret Mead compares family life in India, France, Japan, and Canada, focusing in each case on the upbringing of a one-year-old in a rural setting. Shows how child care—dress, bathing, feeding, discipline—is related to national character. Though dated, a timeless study of enculturation.

3. **Hair Piece**
   1985, 10 mins., color, Women Make Movies
   Clever animated film depicts the dilemma of black women whose hair refuses to fit the standard of beauty of the larger society. Daily ordeals of gels, hot combs, curlers, grease, wigs, creams, and relaxers still do not yield the desired result of hair that "blows in the wind and lets you be free." Lighthearted treatment nonetheless raises serious questions about the effect of prejudice on self-image.

4. **Is It Always Right to Be Right?**
   1970, 8 mins., color, CRM/McGraw Hill Films
   A parable, told by Orson Welles, of a land where people are always

right about everything. Divisions become so great that no one talks to those on the other side, and no one listens, until one day someone admits, "I may be wrong." Initial laughter and shock give way to greater tolerance and a declaration of interdependence.

5. Neighbors
1952, 9 mins., color, International Film Bureau, Inc.
Norman McLaren tells the story of two neighbors who each wish to possess a flower growing on their property line. The resulting dispute escalates until they destroy themselves, their property, and, of course, the flower. No dialogue or narration. Top award winner.

6. Rainbow War
1986, 20 mins., color, Pyramid Film and Video
Allegorical fairy tale of three kingdoms, Blue, Red, and Gold, who have no contact with each other. Fear and rejection of visitors lead to wars, fought aggressively with paint and paintbrushes. Happy ending includes a celebration of new, mixed colors with a rainbow uniting the kingdoms. Produced for Expo 1986; Academy Award nominee.

7. True Colors
1991, 19 mins., color, Coronet/MTI Film and Video
In a powerful segment from the television newsmagazine *Prime Time*, cameras follow two men—one white, one African-American—into the community, from shopping in a retail mall to renting an apartment. Case after case shows that the African American is discriminated against in sometimes overt, sometimes subtle ways. An excellent video for showing the pervasiveness of racism in daily life.

8. Walls and Walls
1973, 9 mins., color, FilmFair Communications
A thought-provoking look at the types of walls people erect to protect themselves from outside intrusion. These include physical barriers such as medieval walled cities, ideological constructs such as flags and religion, and pyschological defenses. Intended to provide safety, the walls can become a prison. Animation, graphics, and live action.

5

Unlearning Stereotypes: New Stories and Histories Emerge

One of the most important goals of multicultural education is to help us move beyond stereotypes to discover a world of human beings with personalities and unique personal histories. Once we know the story of a person or group, once we have attached names to faces, the stereotypes begin to lose validity.

This chapter will begin with a number of excellent films which challenge racial and ethnic stereotypes. They do so by confronting us directly with the distortions, lies, and ugliness of stereotypes. In *Ethnic Notions, Slaying the Dragon*, and *Black History: Lost, Stolen, or Strayed*, stereotypes are so mercilessly exposed as to leave the viewer little choice but to try to discard them forever.

The discussion of stereotypes cannot take place, however, without first acknowledging the role that film—in particular mainstream or Hollywood productions—traditionally has played in instilling in our minds the very stereotypes we now wish to debunk. Among film historians and critics, it is a matter of debate as to whether film actually creates and perpetuates ethnic and racial stereotypes or merely reflects prevailing attitudes. There is little empirical data to prove the case one way or the other, but a survey of film history leaves little doubt that film, at the very least, has contributed to solidifying and reinforcing distorted, racist images.

In study after study, scholars have documented the exploitation and degradation of numerous ethnic, racial, and national groups in American film. (References to some of the major books and articles are provided in the Selected Bibliography.) Film depictions of these groups—from the era of silent cinema to the present—tend invariably to be unflattering, simplistic, and endlessly repetitive. While it goes beyond the scope of this book to discuss these individual histories, one example, that of the Native American, might suffice to give an indication not only of the types of injustices perpetuated, but also of their startling magnitude.

The narrow and erroneous film depictions of Native Americans are detailed in works such as Ralph and Natasha Friar's *The Only Good Indian...The Hollywood Gospel*, Gretchen Bataille and Charles Silet's *The Pretend Indians*, and Michael Hilger's *The American Indian in Film*. The authors show how filmmakers have consistently confused tribes with widely differing customs and cultures or simply blended them into a generic Indian, have falsified their dress and customs, and have bastardized their languages. Moreover, films have been characterized by a fixation on the horsemen of the Plains and Southwest, to the near exclusion of all other tribes, and the only period of interest seems to be the nineteenth-century westward expansion. Can we even think of any urban Indians, any twentieth- century Indians portrayed in film? As John A. Price says:

> Motion pictures have ignored most of that spec-
> tacularly rich cultural diversity of some 560 dif-
> ferent languages and societies in North America.
> Instead, they have portrayed over and over the
> same dozen or so Plains-Southwest tribes that
> acquired enough military prowess to give the
> whites a brief resistance.[1]

As the supreme indignity, Indians have almost exclusively been played by white actors, including Burt Lancaster as Jim Thorpe in *Jim Thorpe, All American* (1951), Sal Mineo in *Tonka* (1958) and *Cheyenne Autumn* (1964), and Donna Reed(!) as Sacagawea in *The Far Horizons* (1955).

The appendix to *The Only Good Indian*, which categorizes films about Indians according to subject, vividly demonstrates how simplistic and widespread the stereotypes have been. The category "Attack on Wagon Train" is a large one, with over seventy films, most of which reinforce the idea that Native Americans were ignorant and bloodthirsty savages impeding the progress of innocent white settlers. Over forty films are listed under the category

"Renegade and/or No Good Indians," over fifty under "Drunken Indians," and over twenty under "Indian Hot Bloods." Titles such as *The Curse of the Red Man, Past Redemption,* and *The Half-Breed's Treachery* suggest the degree of hostility and dehumanization Native Americans were subjected to in these films. Ironically, two categories which suggest that not all Indians are bad actually reveal a patronizing attitude: "Indian, Loyal Friend of Whites" and "Indians Do Good Deeds and Become Good Indians."

For an introduction to how Native Americans and eight other ethnic groups have been treated in the movies, Randall M. Miller's collection of essays in *The Kaleidoscopic Lens: How Hollywood Views Ethnic Groups* is invaluable. In the chapter on Hispanic images in American film, Allen L. Woll discusses how characters are reduced to bandits and lovers. In his essay on Asians in film, Richard A. Oehling shows how the stereotype of the "yellow menace" applies; Asians are depicted as ruthless, clever, and diabolical characters who continually plot the "destruction of America in general and white women in particular."[2] While faring somewhat better, depending on the particular historical circumstances or on the filmmaker, white ethnic groups have also suffered from ugly, limiting stereotypes. Italians are frequently cast as underworld figures; Slavs are depicted as crude, violent, working-class types with strong sexual appetites; and Jews, Germans, and Irish fall into unflattering, set categories.

The depictions of many other countries and cultures—indeed of entire continents and civilizations—have also been reduced to simplistic notions by the movie industry. Has not the enduring image of Africa as a place of jungles and tigers, of savages running naked through the forest screaming and waving spears, been shaped to a large extent by movies? And the image of Arab countries as places where there is nothing but desert, camels, and sheiks?

Given the apparent strength and tenacity of these images and traditions, how might we counter them? What can we do to free ourselves of them in our own minds, to rid ourselves of their hold on our imaginations?

The thesis of this chapter is that we can defuse stereotypes by exposing them. We need to take them apart, analyze them, and inspect them at the same time that we examine our own reactions. Only by understanding how we are manipulated can we begin to resist manipulation. Admittedly, there is one danger in this approach that must not be ignored. If we expose students to stereotypical representations with which they may be unfamiliar, might we not be introducing new prejudices? This danger, however real it may be, seems the lesser of two evils. We run a much greater risk by allowing to go unchallenged the stereotypes which pervade our myths, our popular culture, and our minds.

One of the finest films available for studying stereotypes is *Ethnic Notions: Black People in White Minds*. This exceptional documentary shows how caricatures of blacks have permeated American culture, affecting not only how blacks are perceived by others, but also how they see themselves. According to the film, these caricatures fall into five broad categories: mammy, pickaninny, coon, sambo, and uncle. In cartoons, films, advertisements, greeting cards, songs, children's rhymes, and household artifacts and decorations—such as ashtrays and garden figures—the caricatures have shaped our "most gut-level feelings" about race for over 150 years, well into the middle of the twentieth century. As Barbara Christian from the University of California at Berkeley says, these "notions of the mind" are destructive images: "Our lives are lived under that shadow and sometimes we then even come to believe it ourselves."

The film shows numerous examples of these images and traces them through history. While the images have undergone changes and modifications through the decades, such as the evolution of rural coon to urban coon, they endured in extreme forms into the late 1960s. According to the film, they have served to fix in our minds the ideas that black is ugly, that blacks are savages, and that blacks are happy servants. Even though the extreme images have virtually disappeared, the film emphasizes that they have been replaced by new, more acceptable, variations of the same ideas.

After just one hour, viewers are left stunned and angry at the degree of manipulation to which they have been subjected. The harm done by the cumulative effect of exposure to such images over a century and a half is almost unimaginable.

Significantly, blacks speak to this damage themselves throughout the film in commentary and reflections, both from historical and personal perspectives. Barbara Christian says:

> I have students, both black and white, who believe these images, because it has become a thread throughout the major fiction, film, popular culture, the songs, even the jokes black people make about themselves. It has become a part of our psyche. It's a real indication that one of the best ways of maintaining a system of oppression has to do with the psychological control of people.

Jan Faulkner, from whose collection of memorabilia many of the images and artifacts shown in the film were borrowed, speaks to the distortions of black features, during which the camera focuses on a full view close-up of her face: "My lips don't look like large pieces of liver," she says. "My eyes aren't snow white, or bulging in a frightening appearance."

Because the film tends to leave viewers in a bit of a daze, it may take some time for them to be able to articulate their impressions. Many students will no doubt express shock, surprise, and dismay at the distortions perpetuated for so many decades. You might try to help them to examine their own personal reactions to the grotesque, distorted images. What surprised or angered them particularly and why? Did they find themselves believing any of the stereotypes? Did they find any to be amusing, and, if so, how do they feel about this reaction?

In a mixed group of people of color and whites, you can see how the reactions might differ. Are African Americans more familiar with the images? Less surprised? Do they find the film to be helpful in defusing stereotypes? Do they have any objections to the film?[3] The reactions of African Americans can help the others understand the personal consequences for the victims of stereotyping. At the same time, nonblack students can begin to see how they, too, are hurt and impoverished by accepting falsifications.

Depending on the age of the group, you will find that reactions may vary widely. Older students may well remember seeing and using household artifacts such as those shown in the documentary; they may have grown up with the movies cited; they may be familiar with many, or at least some, of the songs and visual images. Younger students, by contrast, may have limited knowledge of any of the notions presented. For the younger students in particular, follow-up assignments can include watching one of the films mentioned; reading a book such as *Little Black Sambo*; or looking up figures such as T. D. Rice, Thomas Dixon, Al Jolson, Hattie McDaniel, Paul Robeson, Bert Williams, and Ethel Waters.

Since producing *Ethnic Notions*, African-American filmmaker Marlon Riggs has followed with *Tongues Untied*, a view of the lives of gay black men which stirred up much controversy, and the recent *Color Adjustment*, a fascinating look at the depictions of blacks on prime-time television over the past forty years.

Tips for Use: *Ethnic Notions*

To what extent does the idea of "ethnic notions" apply to your own ethnic group? What types of notions, if any, have hurt or offended you personally?

Look at the same sources presented in the film—music, movies, children's books and rhymes, greeting cards, cartoons, and advertisements—to see if the images of mammy, sambo, pickaninny, coon, and uncle still endure in new forms. To what extent are the descendants of these images surviving?

Look at the sources named above to find images that counteract the old stereotypes.

Look for Benetton ads in magazines, or obtain a copy of the publication "United Colors of Benetton" (available in many retail Benetton stores). To what extent do these controversial advertisements dispel stereotypes, and to what extent do they reinforce them?

In the way that both *Ethnic Notions* and *Color Adjustment* expose myths about African Americans, the equally outstanding documentary *Slaying the Dragon* does so for Asian-American women. Interviews with a number of Asian-American women, including actresses Nobu McCarthy and Nancy Kwan, reveal a striking contrast between their self-image and the portrayals of Asian women as exotic, sensual, mysterious creatures in films such as *Sayonara, Teahouse of the August Moon*, and *The World of Suzy Wong*. As Jiyoung Kim, one of the students interviewed in the film, says succinctly, "I'm not like that...Asian women are brought up very strict." Although all the women interviewed resist being identified with the popular images of geisha girls and dragon ladies, they nonetheless cannot easily escape them. As the narrator says, they often find themselves living in the shadow of the Hollywood stereotypes. Television producer Yeh Tung adds: "Being brought up as girls, we're supposed to be passive. And I think that's the dragon that every woman needs to slay."

The damage done by stereotypes to a group's self-image and sense of identity is also illustrated in the 1968 documentary entitled *Black History: Lost, Stolen, or Strayed*. This is a bold and uncompromising look at the "deformed history" of white America and its consequences for blacks. In the introductory segment, narrator Bill Cosby good-naturedly reminds white America of the black historical figures who have never found their way into history books: Matthew Henson, who was Admiral Peary's navigator and the first man to reach the North Pole; Daniel Hale Williams, the first physician to perform open-heart surgery successfully; frontiersman James Beckwourth; inventor Jan Matzeliger; the four black regiments that served with Teddy Roosevelt; and many others.

Cosby strikes a more serious note as he challenges the myth presented in our history books that blacks have come up from slavery. By juxtaposing art works by unknown Africans that served as models or inspirations for astonishingly similar works by Klee, Picasso, and Modigliani, Cosby disputes the notion that during slavery uncultured savages were taken into civilization. In his view, our history has not come to terms with the idea that we didn't take savages from Africa, but human beings, with lives, families, and their own unique cultures.

The consequences of distorted history on the self-image of blacks is vividly demonstrated in the film by a segment comparing drawings made by black children with those of white children. Black children's drawings of trees are often stunted and lifeless, as compared with healthy, leafy trees drawn by whites. In self-portraits, the contrasts are even more telling. Black children often draw themselves with no arms and no hands, revealing their sense of powerlessness. In a study done by psychiatrist Dr. Emmanuel Hammer, who interprets the drawings in the film, blacks are found to draw armless people three times more often than whites. They also draw many faceless people, reflecting a sense of being nobody.

The next segment follows up on the idea of the black person— particularly the black male—being nobody, as Cosby traces the depiction of blacks in films, radio, and television. From the 1915 "vicious anti-Negro" film *Birth of a Nation* to the many films featuring Stepin Fetchit and Bill "Bojangles" Robinson to the productions of well-known series such as *Our Gang* and *Amos 'n' Andy*, Cosby exposes the ever-present, demeaning stereotypes of blacks. Scene after scene shows teeth-chattering, chicken-stealing, crap-shooting blacks who were afraid of gorillas, ghosts, and skeletons. Unable to do much of anything proficiently, they did, however, excel in serving drinks and taking care of white children. Cosby says that even the greats like Robinson had to come into a motion picture through the servants' entrance, as in a master and pet relationship with child star Shirley Temple. And the most recent films, such as those starring Sidney Poitier, fall victim to the new stereotypes which tell the black that he "is nobody unless he joins the white world."

In the final segment of the film, a black teacher uses unusual tactics to help black children learn to assume an equal role in society. He tries to frighten, bribe, bully, and threaten them into accepting insults or agreeing that they are inferior. He thereby challenges them to be confident and defiant in the face of authority, in this case his own authority, when they know that they are right. Cosby asks if this is brainwashing, or if the need for such overcompensation might be understandable in view of the mistreatment of blacks throughout U.S. history.

Black History: Lost, Stolen, or Strayed is a powerful challenge to the mainstream. Because the tone of the film is not accusatory, it has the potential to be heard by those who might otherwise resist its message. Not only is it an eye-opening exposé of the injustices suffered by blacks as they have been systematically written out of history, but it is also a dramatic example of how what is considered to be truth belongs to those in power. Viewers of this film who previously assumed that history is an objective telling of facts are confronted with the shocking realization that our most sacred truths are open to reinterpretation.

Of course, this film was produced some time ago and thus contains none of the recent controversies and developments in multicultural education. In the warm-up, you can explain that the film must be seen as a document of the late 1960s and cannot be expected to address more current issues. Nonetheless, it maintains its value as a way of introducing students to the biases of history perpetuated by dominant groups.

Using Offensive Films

The three films discussed above all include cinematic clips that make use of demeaning stereotypes. Nancy Kwan is seen playing the coy and submissive female, and Shirley Temple talks down to Bill "Bojangles" Robinson. Clearly, these scenes have been selected to illustrate abuses. They are a powerful tool, but they need to be used with great care, so that no one misunderstands and thinks that the film is being shown to advocate the abusive behavior.

Should you choose to select such scenes on your own, the warm-up is extremely important. Students need to know why these particular scenes or films are being shown. Also, certain scenes or films may be so upsetting to certain groups that it may be counterproductive to use them.

To illustrate these points, we can look at an article in the *New York Times* entitled "Nazi Hate Movies Continue to Ignite Fierce Passions" by Rebecca Lieb. She asks whether propaganda films made by the Nazis can still stir up hate: "Are they dangerous or should they be shown? If they are to be shown, who will show them and under what circumstances? Is there anything to be learned from them or are they too horrifying even to contemplate?" Lieb discusses current debate in the United States and Germany over whether *The Eternal Jew*, a "rabidly anti-Semitic" Nazi film, and others of its type should be available to the public or, instead, as the German government and some Jewish groups in the United States believe, should be "kept in vaults, inaccessible to all but a scholarly few."

Significantly, the Anti-Defamation League is opposed to denying access to these films. Lieb reports that the League's research director, Alan Schwartz, is against censoring the films and keeping them under lock and key, but instead calls for "responsible handling of the material."[4]

This responsible handling of the material becomes our charge as multicultural educators. If we decide to use clips from *Birth of a Nation*, for example, students need to be fully aware of the film's troubled history and the massive opposition to it expressed by many blacks since its first showing in 1915. Called "a racist masterpiece" and "possibly the most controversial American film ever released,"[5] *Birth of a Nation* mobilized blacks nationwide to protest its showings and demand its withdrawal. The NAACP's crusade against the film, which lasted half a century, is traced in detail in Thomas Cripps' *Slow Fade to Black*. If the film is to be viewed today, students should know of the strong sentiments it has aroused and of its place in history for blacks: "No longer would blacks be silent while white men in black masks paraded across movie screens."[6]

One way to handle the material responsibly is to show offensive clips as part of a larger unit which includes more sensitive portrayals. In other words, it might be better for the derogatory image not to stand alone, but rather to be compared to and contrasted with more positive images.

As an example of this approach, a fascinating lesson can be built around segments from two films which portray Native Americans in vastly different ways: *Stagecoach*, the 1986 remake of John Ford's 1939 film of the same title, and the documentary *Geronimo and the Apache Resistance*. In the first, Geronimo and his fellow Apaches are depicted in stereotypical fashion. A scene or two, perhaps the opening few minutes and the final battle, should suffice to give students the idea. The opening provides a wonderful example of how the viewer is influenced to take sides against the Indians. We see a romantic view of a lone overland coach making its way across the plains. The accompanying title song, written and sung by Willie Nelson, reinforces the idea that the coach is on an important mission: "We carry precious cargo, we've got precious little time." And the song tells us what we might already suspect: "Geronimo is waiting, there's Apaches on the hill." The scene then moves to a nearby fort, where word comes that Geronimo has just staged an attack in the area: "He killed fourteen men and six women and he's taking scalps." The stagecoach must be warned.

Should you stop the film here, you might fill in the basic plot details which follow. Among the characters on the coach are Doc Holliday, played by Willie Nelson, the Ringo Kid, played by Kris Kristofferson, and Curly, the U.S. Marshal/shotgun guard, played by Johnny Cash. Added to this all-star cast of passengers are two women, one of whom is nine months pregnant. The coach has two stops to make before reaching its destination. At the first stop, it loses its cavalry escorts, since the replacement escorts have been driven off by Apaches. Suspense builds with each stop as the passengers debate whether to turn back. As they leave for the final leg of their journey, they know they must be ready for a battle ahead.

The battle scene is trite and totally predictable. When the U.S. cavalry arrives with bugle and flag just as the situation is looking bleak for the stagecoach, it almost seems a spoof. Of course, whatever sympathies we have at this point are for the people we know on the coach, including, now, a newborn girl. We are not able to identify at all with the faceless Apaches. Interestingly, we are not alone in not knowing the Apaches, as evidenced by this exchange between the Ringo Kid and Curly:

> "You ever know an Apache?"
> "No, never did."
> "Me neither."

When the stagecoach driver seems to talk knowledgeably about Apaches, Curly asks him the same question and receives the same answer.

In *Geronimo and the Apache Resistance*, by contrast, we have the opportunity to get to know something about these people and their lives. You might wish to show several scenes, or, if time permits, the entire documentary. Its stated purpose is to search "for the reality behind the Apache myth," and it does so by allowing the story to be told by direct descendants of Geronimo and his followers. What we learn has nothing to do with the image of "that Apache butcher" from *Stagecoach*, but rather shows a charismatic leader of a brave resistance movement that lasted twenty-five years. We learn that Geronimo was a medicine man, a holy man who suffered a devastating personal blow when marauding Mexican soldiers attacked his camp and killed his wife, mother, and children. We see that he agreed numerous times to peace settlements, but was repeatedly betrayed by the U.S. government. And we hear that he was desperately outnumbered, at one time having only a band of thirty-nine Apaches against 5,000 U.S. cavalry.

When, at the end of the documentary, contemporary Chiricahua Apaches take part in an emotional gathering at Skeleton Canyon, Arizona, the site of Geronimo's final surrender, we gain an inkling of what he represents to them. As the narrator summarizes, "In myth he was an implacable savage, in reality he was a man who risked everything for his home and his way of life."

As a warm-up exercise, you might ask students to write down their associations with Geronimo and the Apaches. After the viewings, you can discuss how they feel about what they wrote. If what they wrote does not fit the stereotypes, where and how did they form their opinions? If what they wrote fits the stereotypes, have they changed their opinions? Has the documentary shattered their stereotypes? Do they believe the documentary? How do they know what to believe? Clearly, the documentary also has its own slant on the truth, and, in any case, represents only one step in the process of searching "for the reality behind the Apache myth." Are students motivated to take that process further? If so, how might they go about it?

Tips for Use: *Geronimo and the Apache Resistance*

Check four or five standard high school or college history textbooks to see how Geronimo is portrayed compared to the film. Do the same with a few standard encyclopedias.

Identify several Native-American place-names in your region, find out what the names mean, and trace their history.

Attend a local Native-American event (powwow, rodeo, arts and crafts show) and write about your experiences. The book *Indian America* by Eagle/Walking Turtle (Santa Fe, NM: John Muir Publications, 1991) is an invaluable resource, providing extensive information on Native-American events held around the country, including a powwow calendar for North America.

Visit an Indian museum, cultural center, or Indian-owned store (addresses provided in *Indian America*). Identify one cultural artifact that especially interests you and look into its significance.

The Myth of the Primitive

Film can also help us challenge the myth, deeply rooted in the American psyche, that technological capability implies overall superiority. Stereotypes of traditional cultures as backward, primitive, and uncivilized have in large part to do with a devaluation of spiritual, intuitive, and nonmaterial values and a corresponding assumption that scientific, technological achievements equal intelligence, virtue, and progress.

A memorable scene from the film *El Norte* questions the assumption that cultures with advanced technology are in possession of the better way. Before showing the scene, which takes about six minutes, you might give a brief sketch of the plot to this point. The focus is on two young Guatemalan refugees, Rosa and her brother Enrique, who faced many hardships in crossing the border to reach Los Angeles and are trying to support themselves as undocumented workers. While still in their home village, they had heard miraculous tales of the technology of the United States—the cars, the refrigerators, and especially the flush toilets. You might wish to show the earlier scene in Guatemala in which the modern technology of the north is seen as the answer to every problem.

The noteworthy scene shows Rosa and her Mexican friend Nacha on their first day of work as housekeepers in the home of an affluent white woman, Mrs. Helen Rogers. Mrs. Rogers explains to them in great detail the settings on the washing machine and dryer, totally confusing her employees and the film viewers, while saying repeatedly that it is all very simple. Left alone with the wash, Rosa tries to push the right buttons, only to be startled by the machine's beeps and other unfriendly noises. Suddenly possessed by an inspiration as she notices the sun shining in from outdoors, Rosa scrubs the laundry clean in the sink, carries it outside, and lays it carefully to dry in the sun as she would do at home. Upon her return, a baffled Mrs. Rogers questions Rosa as to why she would do such a thing and says she simply cannot stand the idea that Rosa would have to do all that scrubbing.

Students might discuss the scene first from the point of view of the employer, who is kind and well-intentioned, but understandably does not want her wash spread out on the lawn. What must she think of Rosa? What do her machines represent to her? How might she relate the incident to her husband that evening? Then the students might look at the scene from Rosa's point of view. What does the machine represent to her? Even if she understood the machine, with its numerous options for fabrics, water level, and rinse cycles, why might she prefer to do wash her way?

The scene is filled with wonderful small details, such as the disdain expressed by Mrs. Rogers when she speaks of scrubbing. From the way she says the word, it is apparent that scrubbing is a demeaning task. Furthermore, she can't imagine that anyone would want to wash by hand: "It's too much work." Rosa, by contrast, seems to have no such preconceptions. As she fills the sink with sudsy water and sets about her work, the image is appealing, almost sensuous. That the physical act of washing clothes could be satisfying would simply not occur to Mrs. Rogers.

Tips for Use: *El Norte*

How does the filmmaker use cinematic elements, such as music, colors, facial expressions, and close-ups, to lend support to Rosa's way?

Examine the failed communication in the two conversations between Mrs. Rogers and her employees. Write a letter to Nacha and Rosa with suggestions for how they might have avoided the misunderstandings. Or, write a letter to Mrs. Rogers with advice as to how she could have been more attuned to what was happening.

Are there newly arrived or immigrant workers you see or come into contact with in your daily life? Where do you see these people? The next time you see such a person, record exactly what thoughts you have about him or her. Then, write down what you imagine the person is thinking at that moment about you.

A similar clash of values between traditional and technological cultures is memorably illustrated in a short section of another film, *River People: Behind the Case of David Sohappy*. Again, because the segment is only five minutes long and is taken from the middle of the film, you might wish to give some background information on Sohappy's struggle to preserve the rights of his people to fish along the Columbia River.

The section in question deals with Celilo Falls on the Columbia River, one of the last traditional fishing villages in the country, which was destroyed in 1957 to make way for a dam. The scene begins with a Department of the Interior film short from the 1930s ushering in the era of hydroelectric power on the Columbia. We learn that "America's conquest of the Columbia has begun" and that "idle resources" will now become "useful goods." We then see extraordinary footage of Celilo Falls as it used to be, with Native-American fishermen perched precariously above the falls and crossing over roaring waters in cable cars. Several Native Americans, including David Sohappy in a voice-over, speak about the days when they still fished Celilo. We then see actual footage of Celilo being dynamited, and the segment ends with a Native-American myth which contains a warning to care for the land.

One way to begin the discussion might be to ask students how they felt as they watched Celilo being dynamited. Did they feel a sense of loss and, if so, why? Did they also feel that something was gained and, if so, what? How can they balance one side against the other? If they had had to make the decision whether or not to destroy the falls, what considerations might have been utmost in their minds?

An interesting exercise might be to replay the film short from the Department of the Interior and have students analyze it. What words are used to persuade the audience that the government is acting in their best interests? How is nature viewed? What values underlie the government's projects along the Columbia?

You might then wish to replay the Indian myth and compare the values expressed here with those of the Department of the Interior. In the myth, the creator takes the sun away because the people "forgot their ways." What are the ways referred to here? How does the sense of what is important in life differ from that of the government film? A comparison of the film and the myth reveals other interesting differences, such as the concept of time. The government film is forward-looking and celebrates change, whereas the myth evokes an ancient world and calls on people to respect the past.

Tips for Use: *River People:*
Behind the Case of David Sohappy

The federal prosecutor in the film says, "Nostalgically, it would be nice if Indians could fish wherever and whenever they want." To what extent do you agree that the River People are clinging to a way of life that is no longer tenable? Should they give up their outdated ways and find new means of support? Or, do you think they are attempting to preserve something invaluable for themselves and for others as well?

Are you aware of the existence of Native Americans in your region or state? Find out where Native Americans are living and do some basic research on their contemporary situation.

Read a Native-American newspaper or journal and write about your impressions. What issues were covered? Was the point of view or writing style different from mainstream publications? What did you learn?

Contact your local politicians to see where they stand on issues affecting Native Americans.

Further Reading
Winterkill, Craig Lesley (New York: Bantam, 1990).

Other Forms of Stereotyping

The films discussed in this chapter provide only a sampling of the countless forms and variations of stereotyping. Depending on your specific purposes and the groups you work with, you will undoubtedly wish to collect your own tapes and clips. If, for example, you work with immigrant groups from Southeast Asia, you might wish to find films which defuse their stereotypes of whites, African Americans, or Hispanic Americans. If you wish to focus on preconceptions of Iranians or Muslims, *Not without My Daughter* is an excellent example of how film can demonize and dehumanize an entire people.

One form of stereotyping that proves especially difficult to dispel is the tendency to lump many different peoples into a single group. How many non-Asian Americans could reasonably distinguish one Asian American from another? Or understand differences between Nicaraguans, Costa Ricans, and Hondurans? Films and film clips which help students begin to make these distinctions, even if the distinctions are at first rather broad, are valuable. The film *The Go Masters* (page 112), for example, can provide American viewers with basic insights into the vast differences between Chinese and Japanese.

Similarly, two short scenes from *El Norte* show that differences in language, dress, appearance, and customs in Central America vary from country to country and from region to region. In the first scene, Enrique learns from an older, experienced friend how to pass as a Mexican. The scene is quite humorous as Enrique practices the necessary slang. In the second scene, Enrique and Rosa attempt to hitch a ride from a truck driver in Mexico, who recognizes instantly that they are not from Oaxaca as they claim.

As you search for materials, you may also find ways to expose seemingly positive stereotypes, such as that of the "model Asian" who excels at everything and outpaces all competition. Recently, Asian Americans have begun to protest against this image, recognizing that it not only creates a backlash of resentment but also prevents help from reaching those who are not succeeding. Furthermore, it can make those Asian Americans whose achievements are less than superior feel like failures.

What kinds of films can be used to expose this type of positive stereotyping? You might begin by acquainting students with the new wave of films made by Asian-American directors. A number of these have been commercial successes, such as Wayne Wang's *Chan Is Missing*, *Dim Sum*, and *Eat a Bowl of Tea* and Peter Wang's *A Great Wall* (page 182). The characters in these films are not superachievers, but ordinary Asian Americans leading normal lives. In *Slaying the Dragon*, Wang speaks about the difficulty he had when making *Dim Sum* not to end up substituting new stereotypes of Asian women for old ones. He says that because filmmakers are "so conscious of trying to portray positive characters for Asians," the characters easily "become cardboards in another way." Wang's portrayal of the mother and daughter in *Dim Sum* is regarded as a breakthrough in creating Asian women characters of depth.

If stereotypes can be challenged in film by showing the other side, by telling new stories, by giving voice to those who have not been heard, then the way we see and relate to each other in our daily lives could indeed be transformed.

Films Discussed

1. **Black History: Lost, Stolen, or Strayed,** 1968, 53 mins., color/b/w, Phoenix/BFA Films and Video.
2. **Chan Is Missing,** 1981, 80 mins., b/w.
3. **Color Adjustment,** 1991, 87 mins., color, California Newsreel.
4. **Dim Sum,** 1984, 87 mins., color, Pacific Arts Video.
5. **Eat a Bowl of Tea,** 1989, 104 mins., color.
6. **El Norte,** 1983, 139 mins., color.
7. **Ethnic Notions,** 1987, 56 mins., color, California Newsreel.
8. **Geronimo and the Apache Resistance,** 1988, 60 mins., color, PBS Video.
9. **River People: Behind the Case of David Sohappy,** 1990, 50 mins., color, Filmakers Library.
10. **Slaying the Dragon,** 1988, 60 mins., color, NAATA CrossCurrent Media.
11. **Stagecoach,** 1986, 100 mins., color.
12. **Where Is Prejudice?,** 1967, 60 mins., b/w, Portland State University and UCEMC. (16mm rental only).

Related Films

1. **Bill Cosby on Prejudice**
   1971, 24 mins., color, Pyramid Film and Video
   As the consummate bigot, Cosby delivers a satiric monologue in which he stereotypes and ridicules every group imaginable.

2. **Black Athena**
   1991, 52 mins., color, California Newsreel
   This examination of Martin Bernal's controversial theory of
   the African origins of Greek civilization brings viewers into the
   midst of current heated debates in the academy surrounding
   Afrocentrism and multicultural curricula. An important film,
   but it takes a scholarly approach and is only useful for viewers
   with prior knowledge of the rather complex historical background.

3. **Black Like Me**
   1964, 110 mins., b/w, Sterling Educational Films, Inc.
   Based on John Howard Griffin's true story of his attempt to
   experience life from a black man's perspective. Having undergone medical treatment to darken temporarily the color of his
   skin, Griffin travels through the Deep South and is subject to
   a sobering degree of humiliation and mistreatment by "fellow"
   whites.

4. **Edward Scissorhands**
   1990, 100 mins., color
   Though the premise seems at first a bit ridiculous, this highly
   original tale of a boy with scissors for hands provides much
   insight into what it means to be different.

5. **Faces of the Enemy**
   1987, 57 mins., color, Catticus Corporation
   Narrator Sam Keen asks why and how people create enemies of
   each other to the point of killing and war. Useful for sensitizing
   students to propaganda and manipulation, but violent and
   heavy, so should be used with care. Also, focus on the U.S./
   Soviet nuclear race now outdated. Based on Keen's book of the
   same title.

6. **The Japanese Version**
   1991, 56 mins., color, Center for New American Media
   Delightful exploration of how the Japanese take Western ideas
   and objects and transform them into their own uniquely
   Japanese version of the original. Humorous, thought-provoking, and perceptive view of how one culture influences another.

7. **Just Black? Multi-Racial Identity**
   1991, 57 mins., color, Filmakers Library
   Sensitive, sometimes lighthearted look at what it means to be
   of mixed racial heritage. Interviews with college students—
   each with a black parent and a white, Asian, or Hispanic
   second parent—reveal some of their difficulties, frustrations,
   and hopes. A challenging film that asks viewers to begin to
   leave old categories of race behind.

8. **Koyaanisqatsi**
   1983, 87 mins., color
   Stunning photography of natural world in its timeless beauty
   juxtaposed with fast-paced, frenetic images of modern, technological society. The film derives its power from the unforgettable contrasts. Splendid musical score, no narration.

9. **My Mother Thought She Was Audrey Hepburn**
   1991, 17 mins., color, Filmakers Library
   Suzanne, a young Asian-American woman, looks with amuse-
   ment and pain at her upbringing in a world of white standards.
   In her attempt to model herself after white women, Suzanne's
   mother has unwittingly engendered "racial self-hatred" in her
   daughter, who now comes to terms with her ethnic identity.

10. **Not without My Daughter**
    1991, 114 mins, color.
    Based on the book by Betty Mahmoody about her own experi-
    ences, the film takes an American woman, played by Sally

Field, on a nightmarish journey to Iran with her Iranian-born husband and young daughter. Originally intending to stay only for a short visit, Mahmoody finds herself trapped in a terrifying world of religious fanaticism. Unable to take her daughter out of the country without her husband's permission, Mahmoody struggles for years as a captive in her husband's home before escaping with her daughter. The portrayal of Islam and virtually all the Iranian characters borders on the demonic.

11. **Race against Prime Time**
    1985, 58 mins., color, California Newsreel
    Disturbing look at how the largely white media misrepresent and stereotype African Americans, using the 1980 Liberty City riots as a case study. Behind-the-scenes visits to the television newrooms of three Miami network affiliates during the riots provide insights into media bias. Though focusing on the situation in 1980, still highly relevant today.

12. **Two Lies**
    1989, 25 mins., b/w, Women Make Movies
    A recently divorced Chinese-American woman undergoes plastic surgery to make her eyes rounder and, thus, more attractive. Her decision leads to a painful confrontation with her teenage daughter, who believes that these two new eyes are two lies.

6

Speaking Different Languages: Verbal and Nonverbal Communication

While all 5.5 billion of us on the planet possess language, we each use it in ways unique to our culture and our individual personalities. Making ourselves understood is often a formidable task even to members of our own culture, let alone to speakers of any of the other 5,000 living languages on earth. The task appears infinitely more complicated, given the fact that verbal facility is only part of what makes for communication. Experts estimate that 60 to 90 percent of what we communicate has nothing to do with words, but rather with nonverbal behavior such as body movement, posture, gestures, facial expressions, and the use of time and space.

The purposes of this chapter are to increase awareness of how languages—both verbal and nonverbal—differ from culture to culture and to illustrate the dynamics of communicating across cultures. By observing what happens when people from different linguistic and cultural backgrounds interact, students can become more attuned to potential dangers and pitfalls. Films which demonstrate misunderstandings are especially useful, but students can also learn a great deal by observing and analyzing successful interactions.

Communication without Words

Because people tend to be intrigued and amused by gestures, the study of gestures is an excellent way to introduce nonverbal communication. The videotape *A World of Gestures* provides an entertaining, thought-provoking look at the way gestures vary around the world. To make the film, students in English as a second language classes at the University of California at Santa Cruz were asked to demonstrate gestures from their home cultures. Their unrehearsed responses lend the film charm and spontaneity.

Beginning with head gestures, Professor Dane Archer leads the international students through a number of categories, including gestures for sex and obscenity, aggression, fear, friendship, love, and suicide. In each case, the differences are astonishing, revealing the infinite ways in which humans speak through motions of their limbs and bodies. The most surprising examples are cases in which the same gesture means different things in different cultures. The good-bye wave in the U.S., for example, means "come here" in Japan, and the sign for "OK" in the U.S. means "money" in Japan, "sex" in Mexico, and "homosexual" in Ethiopia. Also astonishing are cases in which a slight variation in gesture changes the meaning. In England, for example, the "victory" sign is made with the palm facing outward; the same sign with palm facing inward means "screw you."

Prior to viewing the film, you can test to see which gestures are readily recognizable by North Americans. In the instructor's guide, which accompanies the film, Archer suggests that the instructor perform ten gestures, asking the students to write down what each of the gestures means. For example, "shaving" one finger with another means "shame on you"; making a circular motion with one finger at the side of the head means "crazy"; and closing a fist with a raised thumb means "good luck." Students then can grade their fluency in American gestures and discuss the extent to which a knowledge of gestures is pervasive in a culture.

The film raises a number of interesting issues for follow-up discussion. You might first explore how gestures are learned in one's own culture and in a second culture. Are gestures taught explicitly? Are they learned from parents? Teachers? Friends? If there are students from different cultures in the class, they might try to teach each other a gesture unique to their culture. Students will undoubtedly have difficulty associating any emotion or meaning with a new gesture, and they may even find it difficult to imitate and remember the physical movement.

While A *World of Gestures* is particularly useful because of its cross-cultural approach, other films such as *Invisible Walls* and the

Interpersonal Perception Task, which look at nonverbal communication within American culture, can also be used effectively as a first step. Indeed, the idea of nonverbal communication is so new to most students that they may need considerable practice in recognizing otherwise invisible patterns in their own culture before they can compare and contrast across cultures.

Tips for Use: *A World of Gestures*

Spend several hours in a place on campus or in the community where people are coming and going. Observe the nonverbal communication taking place around you.

Tape a television drama and then watch for five or ten minutes with the sound turned off. Speculate about the emotions and content based on nonverbal communication, and make up an appropriate dialogue. Rerun the scenes with sound to see what was really happening.

Watch a foreign film to determine how patterns of nonverbal communication differ from those of your own culture. How would you describe gestures, facial expressions, posture, and dress? How do people greet, touch, and take leave of each other? What can you tell about the way in which people relate to space and to time? How would you describe people's tone of voice? Do they speak loudly or quietly? What about the rhythm and tempo of the language? Do people take turns in conversations? Interrupt each other? Are there noticeable silences?

Fatal Miscommunication

One of the most dramatic illustrations in film of verbal and nonverbal miscommunication is presented in the compelling *The Ballad of Gregorio Cortez*. The entire action—with tragic consequences for both the Anglo and Mexican communities in Texas at the turn of the century—hinges on one scene in which the two sides misread and misinterpret each other's words and intentions. What makes this film so fascinating and useful is that the scene is played out twice—once at the beginning from the perspective of the sheriff's deputy, and again near the end from the perspective of Gregorio Cortez. While the two versions necessarily overlap at certain points, they are so different as to leave the viewer astonished and shaken.

The legend of Gregorio Cortez, as portrayed in the film, begins with a fateful visit by Sheriff W. T. Morris and his deputy, Boone Choate, to Cortez's home in Karnes County, Texas, on June 12, 1901, in search of a horse thief.[1] When the sheriff believes that Gregorio is lying in response to his questioning about a recent horse trade, he tries to make an arrest. A gun battle ensues, with Sheriff Morris first shooting Gregorio's brother Romaldo and then being shot and killed by Gregorio. From this moment on, Gregorio Cortez becomes a fugitive, eluding numerous posses as he makes his way to the border, covering more than four hundred miles on horseback and over one hundred miles on foot, before he is captured on June 22. His reputation as a folk hero lives on in the ballad sung in his memory, a ballad which recurs throughout the film and which, we are informed, is still sung today along the border.

In the first version, the events surrounding the gun battle are told in flashback from the point of view of Boone Choate, who says he can "talk Mexican" and who acts as interpreter. As seen through Choate's eyes, Cortez lies to the sheriff, then resists arrest and murders the sheriff.

The second version is presented much later in the film, in a prison cell, as Gregorio recalls for his attorney and a translator, Señorita Muñoz, the events preceding the shooting. The attorney, upon asking Cortez why he lied to the sheriff about the horse trade, learns from the interpreter that Cortez did not lie, but merely told the sheriff he had traded a *yegua* (mare), not a *caballo* (male horse). Apparently unaware of the distinction in Spanish between the two terms, Choate thought Gregorio was denying having traded a horse at all. When asked by an incredulous Gregorio if this confusion caused his brother's death, the attorney has to admit that it did.

Students may wish to view the entire film on their own, but for classroom purposes you can restrict the showing to the two clips in question.[2] You will undoubtedly want to stop the tape at the end of the first clip to discuss the occurrences. At this point, you can determine the extent to which the students' perceptions of what happens coincide with Choate's. In large part, this will depend on the students' knowledge of Spanish, since Choate's translations—both of the sheriff's questions and of the Cortez brothers' responses—are inaccurate and tainted by malevolence. For those who do not know Spanish, however, this misrepresentation would not be apparent. For example, those not knowing Spanish will probably believe Choate that Gregorio is indeed resisting arrest when Choate tells the sheriff, "He says no man can arrest him." Gregorio has not said this, however, but merely asked in Spanish why he is being arrested when he has not done anything wrong.

After seeing the second clip, students will undoubtedly be struck by the difference in moods in the two parallel scenes leading up to the shooting. As oppposed to the grim feeling of foreboding felt by the viewer as the sheriff and Choate approach the ranch in the first version, Gregorio in the second version takes us back to an idyllic domestic scene. It is late afternoon, his children are playing, and Gregorio is sitting outside with his face full of lather as his wife shaves his beard. The rays of the sun on his face, a gentle wind in his wife's hair, and the sound of a rooster crowing in the yard make for a tranquil, sensuous mood. Background guitar music, which reinforces this mood, abruptly stops with the sound of hoofbeats, a clear sign of danger and intrusion.

Lulled into tranquillity by the scene, the viewer now sees events from the Mexican family's side. We watch Gregorio, fearful of the strangers, trying to protect his wife and children. We observe his confusion as he tries to respond to the sheriff's questions, then his horror as the sheriff pulls out his gun and shoots Romaldo. The events all seem to happen very quickly, probably reflecting Gregorio's panic that the situation is out of his control. (The first version, told from the point of view of those in control, seemed to transpire more slowly. Also, in the first version we saw Gregorio and his family only from a distance, whereas now the camera gives us close-ups of their faces, leaving the sheriff and Choate alienated from us in long shots.)

Students can also analyze the nonverbal communication which precedes the shooting in both versions. Who seems to be threatening whom? What movements, gestures, facial expressions seem friendly or hostile? How does the filmmaker lead the viewer to perceive danger?

Another interesting point of comparison is the role of the translators. For Spanish speakers especially, it is revealing to compare the behavior and abilities of the two, one of whom is incompetent and antagonistic toward Cortez, the other highly competent and sympathetic toward him. Spanish speakers will note how poorly Choate speaks and understands Spanish; he does not even ask "What's your name?" properly, and the nuances of the Cortez brothers' responses are lost on him. He uses the familiar *tu* form of address, whereas Señorita Muñoz uses *usted* and often addresses Cortez respectfully as "Señor" or "Señor Cortez." She is careful to convey not only Cortez's words, but his tone and feelings.

As important as the linguistic and nonverbal miscommunication may be, these two scenes show that the reasons for the violence are much more profound. They demonstrate what is stated in the opening credits: that the film deals with "two cultures—the Anglo and the Mexican—living side by side in a state of tension and fear."

That this tension and fear need not lead inevitably to confrontation is demonstrated in another scene of the film, a short episode between the exhausted fugitive Cortez and an Anglo cowboy he encounters in isolated countryside. Though neither speaks the other's language, and both are wary of the other at first, the two men manage to communicate sufficiently to approach each other. Cortez shares the cowboy's meal, listens as the cowboy talks to him in English, and falls asleep for the night. Students might interpret what signals the two strangers give to each other—verbally and nonverbally—to forge a temporary bond of trust and companionship.

Take Two

The idea of looking at the same interaction from two different perspectives is also explored in an instructional video entitled *Take*

Two. Filmed in 1982 by the Intercultural Relations Institute at Stanford University as a tool for teaching English, it shows four different vignettes, each between a native and a nonnative English speaker. In each case, communication fails the first time through, but then the scene is replayed, and in the second take, the two conversants do a better job.

The video itself is not of the best technical quality—it has a homemade feel and is difficult to understand at times—but the idea behind it is quite ingenious. You will want to preview it in its entirety but probably should show only one or two scenes to the group. The best of the four is the one between Anh from Vietnam and an American classmate who tries to engage her in conversation. In the first take, the American tries to be friendly, but ends up frustrated with Anh's monosyllabic answers and lack of reciprocity. In a follow-up interview with Anh, we learn that she, too, was frustrated by the barrage of questions she faced, feeling that she had no time to think or to answer. Both young women say afterwards that they felt very uncomfortable and were looking for a way out of the conversation, even though they would have liked to get to know each other. In the second take, Anh tries to give more complete answers and ask questions herself, and her American counterpart also seems to relax a bit. They end up agreeing to get together to play Ping-Pong.

The value of the take-two approach lies in helping students learn how to analyze their communication patterns. The scenes vividly show that when communication fails, both sides need to reflect and adjust. Rather than relying on the video itself, however, you can use the take-two format and have students invent their own skits to demonstrate specific cross-cultural communication skills. For example, the skill demonstrated in the scene between Anh and the American is how to maintain conversation. In another vignette between a Japanese translator and her employer, the skill demonstrated is interactive listening; in the first take, Michiko misunderstands the instructions and carries out the wrong task, but in the retake, she is able to ask for clarification, interrupt when she is confused, and check that she has understood.

In their own skits, students might demonstrate a wide variety of different skills. They can, for example, devise a skit in which a person's accent is difficult to understand. Or they can devise a skit in which a person from a culture that tends toward indirect communication is confronted with a direct American. Whatever the case, students should consider both verbal and nonverbal communication as they create their skits.

Tips for Use: *Take Two*

If you have ever spoken a foreign language with native speakers, how did it feel? What did you learn about accents and communication?

Is English a second language to any family member or friend? Interview this person about the difficulties he or she has encountered in communicating. What have the frustrations and rewards been?

Visit an ESL class on your campus or in the community. Who are the students? What were your impressions of the class?

Visit a bilingual school in your area. Who are the students and who are the teachers? How is the instruction handled in two languages? What were your impressions of the visit?

Different Englishes

The BBC production *Crosstalk* is an eye-opening film that, like *Take Two*, shows how English speakers from different cultural backgrounds can totally misinterpret what the other is saying. In excerpts from several real-life situations, we see how people who seem to begin an interaction with goodwill and "no conscious racial hostility" end up irritated and frustrated.

The film makes the point that even the most ordinary exchange can be fraught with difficulty. This is demonstrated in a bank scene, in which an Indian customer, Mr. Sandhu, wishes simply to deposit money. He uses almost exactly the same words as a British customer desiring the same transaction, but his different tone and intonation cause problems. When the British teller hands him a form to fill out, for example, Mr. Sandhu says, "No, no. This is the *wrong* one." The emphasis on the accusatory word "wrong" as well as a number of other unexpected tones carefully analyzed in the film causes the teller to respond with annoyance: "Well, why didn't you say so in the first place?"

This short scene and the narrator's analysis can be enormously instructive to all English speakers. What apparently is a normal speech pattern for an Indian speaker of English and not meant to be impolite in the least is interpreted by the British speaker as pushy and accusatory. Significantly, the teller is not aware of why he is becoming annoyed. He might falsely draw inferences about the Indian's character simply because his English ear is unaccustomed to the way the Indian's voice rises and falls.

In a more extensive scene, the same unfortunate Mr. Sandhu, who has been living in England for fourteen years, is shown at an interview for a position as a college librarian. Mr. Sandhu is highly qualified for the position and desperately needs a job, but the interview is a disaster almost from the start. The three British interviewers interpret Mr. Sandhu's answers as evasive and imprecise, whereas Mr. Sandhu is simply following his own cultural norms about how to structure and present information. The interviewers also misconstrue his honesty about why he is applying for this particular position as reflecting a lack of interest in their college.

The scene is painful to watch. As the interview deteriorates, and as both sides show mounting impatience and tension, the viewer also feels frustrated by the obvious miscommunication in a situation of such critical importance to Mr. Sandhu.

You might stop the film after the scene and ask the students how the misunderstandings could have been avoided. What could Mr. Sandhu or the interviewers have done differently? For example, when Mr. Sandhu produces his certificates of qualification, the interviewers might have looked at them, or they might at least have inquired as to whether it is common practice in India to bring certificates to an interview, explaining that in England this is not customary. A willingness to address the issue might have prevented

Mr. Sandhu's feeling of rejection when his certificates did not seem to be of interest. After discussing possible ways to improve the communication, students might try role playing the scene in an attempt to achieve a more constructive outcome.

At the end of the film, six suggestions are offered for improved interethnic communication. Although the last two—listening until the other person has finished talking and allowing extra time—are obviously useful and important, the others are more problematic. For example, the suggestion to talk openly about discrimination may or may not be a good idea, depending on the particular circumstances. In any case, the six suggestions should be examined and discussed rather than automatically accepted.

Despite its enormous value, *Crosstalk* does have some shortcomings which you might wish to bring out in the warm-up. The film was made in 1982 and has the appearance of being a bit outdated. At first glance, it might seem to apply only to the multiracial situation in England, whereas its message is actually much broader. Its first scene, which takes place in a social worker's office, may be difficult for Americans to understand, since the misunderstandings stem, at least in part, from an Indian's confusion over the difference between social security and unemployment benefits in England.

But the importance of the film's message far outweighs these difficulties. *Crosstalk* shows us something we might never otherwise become aware of—the "unrecognized conventions" and "hidden mechanisms" of speech, which have the potential to undermine communication and confirm stereotypes. Particularly as English becomes a world language, native and nonnative speakers alike benefit from realizing that there are many Englishes and that the cultures behind these Englishes vary widely. The more we are able to recognize those differences, the less likely we are to be disturbed and alienated by English usage different from our own. Thus the film can be used effectively not only in ESL classes, where the students will be able to relate to the problems from their own experience, but in any group attempting to develop intercultural communication skills.

A very different type of failed communication among speakers of English can be explored in the memorable *The Long Walk Home*. The film focuses on two women, a black domestic worker, Odessa Cotter, and her white employer, Miriam Thompson, who is driving Odessa to and from work during the Montgomery, Alabama bus boycott in 1955 (see chapter 10 for further discussion of this film, including warm-up suggestions). In a revealing episode during Christmas dinner, we see how inequities in power restrict and inhibit communication.

As the scene opens, Odessa and Claudia, a coworker, are in the process of serving dinner to the large family when a conversation about the boycott starts. Odessa comes in from the kitchen as Miriam's mother contributes her opinion: "These niggers just want too much and they're not willing to work for it." Odessa offers the mother some dinner rolls and continues offering rolls around the table to an awkward silence, interrupted only by the mother's self-defense: "Well, that's the way I feel. I don't care who hears me."

The scene continues as Norman Thompson, Miriam's husband, goes into the kitchen to give Odessa and Claudia Christmas bonus checks and to ask them a few questions. Unaware that his wife is driving Odessa the considerable distance she has to travel to work, he asks Odessa how she is getting back and forth and how she feels about the boycott. Carefully protecting Miriam and guarding her own feelings—which would surely offend her employer—Odessa gives answers which are truthful but reveal little.

You might wish to stop the tape at this point to analyze the communication. First, what happens around the dinner table? What does Odessa communicate to the guests by her behavior and how? Clearly, her silence and extreme propriety show feelings she is not allowed to verbalize. What is Odessa thinking? What might she have said if she were not in a powerless position? You can also examine the reactions of the family. What is the group saying to Odessa by *their* silence? Is the group united, or does anyone show suppport for Odessa? What is Miriam thinking?

Similarly, you can analyze the scene in the kitchen to see what is really being communicated. Does Mr. Thompson want to know the truth about how Odessa feels? How does his verbal and nonverbal behavior set the tone for a superficial exchange? For her part, how does Odesssa manage to deflect Thompson's questions so adroitly? What verbal and nonverbal signals does she use to discourage him from continuing the conversation? How does she feel and what is she thinking? What is Claudia thinking? What would Thompson have had to do to engage Odessa in real conversation?

Once you have looked at some of these questions, you can play the next scene, in which Odessa and Claudia leave the house and talk for a moment before heading home. Now their true feelings about the two encounters come out, and their manner of speaking is totally different. They are animated, relaxed, and informal. Their demeanor contrasts sharply with the reserve and caution displayed in the Thompsons' home. They almost seem to be two different people. What they say to each other—and how they say it—is a world apart from the way they interact with the Thompsons.

Films Discussed

1. **The Ballad of Gregorio Cortez,** 1982, 99 mins., color.
2. **Crosstalk,** 1982, 30 mins., color, Films, Inc. (rental UCEMC).
3. **Interpersonal Perception Task,** 1987, 40 mins., color, UCEMC.
4. **Invisible Walls,** 1969, 12 mins., color/bw, UCEMC.
5. **The Long Walk Home,** 1990, 98 mins., color.
6. **Take Two,** 1982, 40 mins., color, Intercultural Relations Institute.
7. **A World of Gestures,** 1991, 28 mins., color, UCEMC.

Related Films

1. **Bilingual Education: An Inside View**
   1985, 25 mins., color, UCEMC
   Scenes of bilingual classrooms provide a glimpse into how instruction is handled in two languages. Children, teachers, and administrators voice their opinions on bilingual education.

2. **Becoming Bilingual** (2 parts)
1991, 80 mins., color, UCEMC
First part, *Ambos a Dos*, follows the progress of Nicole Verdejo, a third-grader from Puerto Rico, in a bilingual school in East Harlem. The school's "maintenance" program helps her to remain fluent in Spanish while providing a transition into the new language. The second part, *Newtown High*, shows how 4,000 high school students speaking nearly fifty different languages are carefully guided through a "transition" language program. Various approaches to bilingual education are presented, and some of the controversies are discussed.

3. **Rassias in China**
1991, 60 mins., color, offered by Dartmouth College (through 1-800-952-OVEN or PO Box 952-OVEN, Norwich, VT 05055) When renowned Dartmouth College professor John Rassias takes his unique methods for teaching foreign languages to Beijing, American and Chinese cultures meet in unexpected ways. A remarkable film that explores profound questions about the process of encountering a second language and culture.

4. **Straight Up Rappin'**
1992, 29 mins., color, Filmakers Library
A memorable introduction to the performers and lyrics of rap. Amateurs, from young boys who rap about the Bill of Rights to a woman who raps about revolution, impress not only with their art form, but their political stance. Makes street poetry accessible, and even appealing, to those who may tend to dismiss it.

5. **You Must Have Been a Bilingual Baby**
1991, 46 mins., color, Filmakers Library
Narrator David Suzuki looks at the process of second-language acquisition on the part of infants and toddlers, children in bilingual schools, and adults taking classes. Especially interesting segment on the "bilingual brains" of interpreters.

7

Great Walls of Difference: The International Arena

Though many nations recognize the increasingly urgent need for international cooperation and unity, conflict nonetheless continues to dominate the world picture. Situations of long-standing strife, such as that between Arab and Jew in the Middle East, seem intractable, offering only glimmers of hope for improvement or eventual resolution. In other equally desperate conflicts, such as the seemingly unending struggle of black South Africans against the apartheid regime, change is occurring, though the future is still uncertain. Wherever one looks in the world, old clashes and newer eruptions of ethnic and national tensions raise fundamental questions as to the feasibility of different peoples coexisting peacefully as neighbors, much less living in harmony under one government.

For American students, these crises involving peoples and nations, however monumental they may be, can seem remote and impersonal. It is often hard to relate to people one does not know, to places where one has never been. What film can do is bring the people and their stories to life. From the films discussed in this chapter, students can gain an insight into the nature of cultural conflict around the world, including the huge gaps in understanding that exist between people in developed and developing countries. They can begin to understand what types of great walls divide peoples of the world from each other, and from us.

The Ancient Clash of Arab and Jew

A conflict in the international arena that is familiar to many Americans, and seems almost the archetype of cultural hatred, is the bitter struggle between Arabs and Jews in Israel. Robert

Gardner's 1989 documentary *Arab and Jew: Wounded Spirits in a Promised Land*, based on David Shipler's book of the same title,[1] is a compelling, extraordinarily evenhanded presentation of both sides of the conflict. Its focus is the "psychological landscape where Arabs and Jews meet," and it explores the question of how each side views the other.

In the first part of the documentary, the modern-day history of these two "ancient faiths" with their "ancient hatreds" is traced from the time of the British Mandate, starting in 1920, through six recent wars to the present. The history comes alive not only through the beautifully written narrative, presented by Shipler himself, and the stunning photography of Israel, but also through the eloquent personal testimony of numerous Arabs and Jews. The history is told by those who have lived and suffered it—war veterans, journalists, teachers, religious leaders, West Bank settlers—and by the young people who now inherit its wounds.

Tips for Use: *Arab and Jew: Wounded Spirits in a Promised Land*

Before viewing the film, write down the first things that come to mind in association with the following: Arab, Palestinian, Jew, Zionist, Israel, Middle East. Then consider, after the film, how your ideas have been changed or modified.

Dozens of fascinating people from many walks of life appear in this documentary. Whom would you most like to meet in real life and why? Or whom would you least like to meet and why?

Invite a representative from a local synagogue or from a group such as the Anti-Defamation League to visit the class to present views on the contemporary situation in Israel. Invite someone to present the Palestinian viewpoint as well.

Clip articles from the press over a period of weeks to see how the Arab/Israeli conflict is being presented.

These personal voices from both sides of the historical events bring out the enormous complexity and intensity of the issues. The

Deir Yassin massacre, the 1948 Arab exodus to neighboring countries, the occupation of the West Bank and Gaza are all seen from both the Jewish and Arab perspectives. In case after case, extreme polarization defines the positions. For example, what is viewed by Rabbi David Hartman as naked terrorism, seems an armed struggle for liberation to a young Palestinian activist called Josef, who was only one year old when the West Bank was captured and who spent four years in prison.

In describing the situation, Palestinian journalist Jamil Hamad uses the words of Chaim Weizmann, Israel's first president, who said that the clash is not between right and wrong, but "between two rights." Both Jews and Palestinians belong to national movements with historical rights to the same land. Both have an "ideology of return" as part of their deepest purpose. Jews say, "We've come back here because we never left here."A Palestinian voice says that when you lose your land, "it could kill your spirit."

Each side, convinced that it alone is in the right, holds a "complicated set of prejudices" about the other. The second part of the film focuses on these prejudices, showing how they permeate the language, the literature, and the minds of people. As possessors and occupiers of the land, the Jews tend to think of the Arabs as disloyal, primitive, dirty, and cunning. The Arabs, an underclass whether living as noncitizens in the occupied and disputed territories or as Israeli citizens in other parts of the country, tend to think of the Jews as arrogant, authoritarian, and greedy. On both sides hatred and fear abound.

At the end of the film, hope is expressed in the form of "small but important countercurrents," such as a program in both elementary and high schools that offers Arab and Jewish students the opportunity to visit each other. Jewish teacher Ori Geva describes a highly emotional encounter during one of these visits in which a Jewish girl finally breaks down in sobs upon realizing that an Arab pupil would be willing to see her badly hurt in a PLO terrorist attack. Her reaction and that of her classmates—who also begin to weep— cause the young Arab boy to see a Jew as a person for the first time and thus to question his own radical position, formed purely on the basis of abstractions.

What the many people interviewed in the film seem to have in common is their pain. While it is pain that divides them, it may ironically be this very pain that can help to bring them together. Rabbi Josef Porat, who lost his daughter Tirza in a violent encounter between Jews and Arabs, is prepared to begin the process of healing: "If a tree is uprooted," he says, "you must plant one. It doesn't help to uproot your enemy's tree. It is no solution." And the narrator ends the film with the idea that peace is only to be found by looking at each other and rediscovering each other's humanity: "They will not escape from one another. They will not find peace in treaties or victories. They will find it, if at all, by looking into each other's eyes."

The Wall of the Law in South Africa

The most extreme example of a barrier dividing peoples in today's world may be the system of apartheid in South Africa. That this government-sanctioned form of racism has survived into the 1990s can only be viewed as a mark of shame in our modern age. One way to sensitize students to South Africa's recent history and at the same time help them look more carefully at the type of information they are getting is to compare the antiapartheid feature film *Cry Freedom*, made outside the country by white director Richard Attenborough, with the South African production *Mapantsula*.

Cry Freedom, the true story of a unique friendship between two South Africans—black leader Stephen Biko and white newspaper editor Donald Woods—is a laudable accomplishment. It puts the political system of apartheid into personal terms, offering a profoundly disturbing glimpse into the damage apartheid does to whites and blacks alike. It captures the charisma and humanity of the legendary Biko and brings his brutalization and murder at the hands of the government to a world audience. And it achieves what Attenborough wanted it to do, namely to become part of the worldwide protest against what he calls the obscene system of apartheid.[2]

Cry Freedom is an excellent tool for introducing students to the perspectives of both black and white South Africans and to the possibilities for alliances and joint action. What the film does not do, however, is place the blacks in the center of their own cause. Even a figure as fascinating and monumental as Biko is not allowed to carry the film, but incredibly his story is made secondary to the main plot surrounding Donald Woods. Biko's death takes place quite early in the film, leaving the rest of the film to feature Woods and his family—the threats and dangers they face, the agonizing decisions they must make, and their ultimate triumph.

This objection need not detract from the extraordinary conviction and sacrifice of Donald Woods, who at great personal risk supports Biko and who, after Biko's death, decides to undertake an escape from South Africa with his wife and five children for the sake of publishing Biko's biography. The question that you might pursue with students, however, is why Attenborough made the decision to weight his story in favor of Woods. Was he simply more interested in the Woods' family story than in that of Biko and his family? Was he unable as a white director to appreciate fully the black perspective? Did he suspect that mostly white theater audiences would relate more readily to the material as seen through the eyes of whites? Or was he perhaps forced by financial considerations to avoid a primarily black depiction? In the introduction to *Cry Freedom: A Pictorial Record*, Attenborough offers a clue to his thinking:

> Film financiers, in the main, are nervous of any subject of real substance. They are convinced that audiences around the world wish only to be "entertained" and that anything which challenges their views or engages their intelligence as well as their hearts is a potentially dangerous box office proposition.[3]

An examination of other antiapartheid feature films shows the same tendency to focus on the struggles and achievements of white liberals rather than of black South Africans. *A World Apart*, by

British director Chris Menges, is a moving story of the insidious effects apartheid has on people's most private lives. Based on the true story of white journalist Ruth First, it shows how First's daughter Molly comes to terms with her mother's activism against apartheid and her extended detention. In *A Dry White Season*, black director Euzhan Palcy from Martinique also focuses on a white protagonist, the schoolteacher Ben du Toit, who is transformed from an unquestioning participant in the apartheid system to a committed opponent.

The extraordinary 1988 South African production *Mapantsula* distinguishes itself from the three discussed above by telling the story from the inside. With this film, you will need to provide careful warm-up because it does not easily lend itself to Western viewers with limited knowledge of apartheid. Above all, students need to know that the movie was filmed by two South Africans, Thomas Mogotlane, who is black, and Oliver Schmitz, who is white, under the pretense of making an apolitical gangster movie. The antiapartheid theme would not have been tolerated by the government authorities, as proven by the fact that the film was later banned from theatrical distribution; the South African Censor Board said that it "could have dangerous political effects" and might "incite the viewers to violence." In the Board's view, the film communicates a "clear message: refuse cooperation with the authorities and side with the rebellious elements in black society."[4]

With this knowledge, students can appreciate the ingenuity of directors who had to create a film on two levels: an innocuous gangster story and a political statement. In the warm-up, you should also introduce students to the four languages of the film (English, Zulu, Sotho, and Afrikaans) and to the basics of the plot, which takes place in flashbacks from a jail cell and can be difficult to follow.

Basically, *Mapantsula*, a Zulu word for petty criminal, is the story of Panic, a hoodlum who has no ambitions other than to look out for himself and to steal enough money to pay for his flashy clothes and nighttime carousing. As the film progresses, the intolerable conditions of daily life in the township are such that the people around Panic—including his woman friend Pat, a domestic worker who joins the movement after she is unjustly fired—are all drawn into the struggle against the government. While sharing a jail cell with a group of political activists who despise him, Panic realizes he can no longer avoid responsibility. Refusing to continue as a police informer, the role he has adopted in prison, he finally takes a defiant stand against the oppressive system.

As students compare *Mapantsula* with *Cry Freedom*, they will certainly mention that *Mapantsula* has a different feel to it, probably because it is filmed inside the township of Soweto and in Johannesburg, rather than in Zimbabwe, the location of *Cry Freedom*. They may note that the actors are black South Africans, including Thomas Mogotlane himself in the title role, rather than outsiders. Though Denzel Washington does a superb job as Stephen Biko in *Cry Freedom*, he is not South African, nor does he resemble Biko in physical characteristics. Moreover, a comparison of themes will reveal that *Mapantsula* focuses on the political consciousness not of a leader or hero but of an ordinary person. According to these South African film directors, the story of Panic puts the struggle where it belongs—with the common people. *Mapantsula* shows that no one can remain indifferent, for the conditions require that all people—regardless of personality, background, or education—find their way to political commitment.

You can also explore with students sensitive questions regarding the point of view of the insider vs. the outsider. How legitimate is it for Attenborough and other outsiders to tell the story of apartheid, particularly if they choose the point of view of white liberals? Does this perspective provide the best access to the issues for largely white audiences? Should they be exposed to films like *Mapantsula* as well, or is this film too alien to their experiences? Would *Mapantsula* be a "dangerous box office proposition," as Attenborough suggests? Finally, what about the question of balance? Undeniably, white liberals have made important contributions to the struggle against apartheid, and their stories should be told. But what if these are the only stories we get? What types of inequities are created by a focus on this single perspective?

The Boat Is Full: Refugees in Crisis

Perhaps the greatest challenge to the worldwide system of walls and barriers between sovereign nations is the current refugee crisis. The number of refugees driven from their homes—whether by reason of economic hardship, political turmoil and persecution, famine, war, or natural disasters—has reached staggering proportions. An estimated eighteen million people have left their countries, and another approximately twenty million are displaced within their own countries. Drastic as the numbers appear, the situation is made more desperate when one realizes that millions of the refugees are children, and many of the adults have been refugees their entire lives.

As refugees worldwide attempt to resettle and find new lives, many look for help to nations such as the United States and Canada, long regarded as havens for the politically and economically oppressed. A highly critical look at Canada's immigration policies is provided in the extraordinary documentary *Who Gets In?*, produced by the National Film Board of Canada. In careful, vivid detail, the documentary shows how Canada's current policies are based primarily on self-interest, not on humanitarian principles.

In an attempt to answer the question, "What does it take to become a Canadian?" the film focuses on a typical developing world immigration outpost in Nairobi, Kenya. Here Mike Malloy, senior immigration officer at the Canadian High Commission, sees himself charged with finding "good people" and "keep[ing] the rascals out." What becomes increasingly evident is that "good people" are defined in exceedingly narrow terms. If applicants have no close relatives living in Canada and thus must apply as "independents," they must prove not only that they are in fear for their lives, unable to return home, and unable to stay in the present location, but, above all, that they are "suitable" for life in Canada. As Malloy says, the immigrants will ultimately find themselves living in Canadian neighborhoods, and they have to fit in. When considering applicants, he asks himself, "If this person moves in next to my mom, what's she going to think about it?" This type of thinking seems to leave the door wide open for racial preference, if not outright discrimination.

Of the various cases Malloy handles in the film, all of which are profoundly disturbing, the most unsettling is the one of a man from Zaire named George, who is the target of a manhunt by his government. As a special security guard in Zaire, George was in charge of fifteen political prisoners who were arrested for trying to organize an official opposition. On the eve of their execution, George managed to set them free, as he says, in the name of human rights. Having escaped from Zaire to a Kenyan refugee camp, George has been able to learn quite respectable English in his seven months in the camp, which Malloy himself admits is "really remarkable." He is impressed with George's case, but makes a puzzling statement that perhaps George should spend a "couple years growing tomatoes or something" before emigrating. A year after his interview with Malloy, George is refused entrance into Canada on the grounds of personal unsuitability.

Similarly, student activists in Kenya, many of whom have been arrested and tortured by the government of Daniel arap Moi, stand virtually no chance of even being heard by Malloy, since Canada does not want to jeopardize its good relations with Kenya or risk having to relocate its immigration post. Responsible for a population of three million refugees, Malloy and his staff of two end up approving only three hundred applicants a year. It is clear, the narrator summarizes, that "Africans don't seem to have what Canada wants."

Explaining that Canada, with its declining birth rate, does need people, if not Africans, the documentary now changes scene to Hong Kong, "an immigration officer's dream." To entice and accommodate the large number of successful entrepreneurs desiring to leave this tiny island before it is returned to mainland China in 1997, Canada has stationed no fewer than thirteen immigration officers there. An interview with a senior advertising executive and his wife, who have assets of $400,000, offers a sharp contrast to Malloy's intense screening. The couple is literally wooed, since they are in a position to "come to a city like Toronto, buy a house in an upscale neighborhood, and start paying taxes tomorrow." As the immigration officer tells them, "With your background, they're dying to snap you up."

At the time the documentary was made, the Hong Kong immigration post had become Canada's largest, approving one of every five new Canadians. The rules here are different from those applied in Africa. Applicants can emigrate to Canada as investors if they are willing to invest at least 250,000 Canadian dollars, as retirees if they are worth at least $300,000, and as entrepreneurs if they are worth at least $100,000. What is striking about the interviews here are the questions that do not get raised about applicants' personal lives and backgrounds. It is not even necessary to speak the language or to resolve problems with an application oneself, since Canadian immigration lawyers can fly over to represent applicants for about $8,000 per case. The rationale for this immigration policy is simple: these people create wealth, jobs, and opportunities for Canadians. As Mike Malloy says, "You really can never get enough of people with that type of entrepreneurial spirit."

At the end, the narrator poses directly the troubling questions raised by the documentary. If Canada's immigration policy is now favoring those who already possess money, class, and privilege, where will that leave people who have only the "traditional immigrant virtue" to offer—a willingness to work hard? Where will that leave those who are prepared to "start at the bottom, sacrifice, [and] persist," those who "built Canada in the first place?" Indeed, the unavoidable irony of the situation is that "most of Canada's immigrant ancestors wouldn't get in today," nor would most native Canadians.

Though aimed at the situation in Canada, the film's questions apply equally to the United States, also a nation of immigrants with an enduring belief in the value of offering refuge to those in need. *Who Gets In?* will undoubtedly arouse strong emotions in your students, since the reality it presents conflicts so harshly with the deep-seated traditions and values of most Americans. While U.S. students will no doubt wish to think about the ethics of Canada's position, the film also provides a powerful incentive for them to investigate our own policies. Is the United States going in the same direction as Canada? What are our current immigration policies and how are they decided? Who gets in here? How ethical and equitable does our own system seem to be? What are the moral dilemmas one might face in developing criteria for immigration?

Tips for Use: *Who Gets In?*

Before viewing the film, write down what you imagine the three most important criteria to be for admission to the United States as an immigrant.

What does a person have to do to become a citizen of the United States? What do you think of this process?

How does U.S. immigration policy affect life in your own town, city, or state? Is there an effect on your personal life?

Invite a representative from the Immigration and Naturalization Service (INS) to speak with your class on current immigration policy. Try to determine how U.S. policy compares to the film's presentation of immigration policy in Canada.

Do you know anyone who has immigrated to the United States? Find out their impressions of the immigration process.

Imagine that you are consultants asked to advise INS on reforming immigration policy. In small groups, develop a list of your criteria for acceptance into this country.

A look at the past likewise reveals that U.S. immigration policies have not always held to the ideals of welcoming the "huddled masses yearning to be free." The poignant documentary *Carved in Silence* tells a story of immigration different from our national myth, a story which took place on the side of the ocean where immigrants found "no Statue of Liberty greeting them." On Angel Island, in the middle of San Francisco Bay, hopeful immigrants were imprisoned—sometimes for years—for no reason other than their Chinese nationality. Interviews with those who experienced detention on Angel Island over fifty years ago bring this sorrowful chapter of American history to life. One man says he will never forget what happened on the island, "where our pain was carved in silence."

Indeed, on the walls of the cells can still be seen Chinese characters—anonymous poems of hope and despair painstakingly etched into the stone.[5]

Because the crisis of refugees, whatever the time and place, so easily remains an abstraction to others and because numbers like eighteen million quickly lose their meaning, feature films which tell individual stories help students to develop empathy and to question national and international policy. The Swiss film *The Boat Is Full* shows the desperate circumstances faced by a group of Jewish refugees from Hitler as well as by the Swiss family that shelters them during a time when Switzerland had virtually closed its borders to fleeing Jews. A second Swiss film, the Oscar-winning *Journey of Hope*, focuses on the act of flight itself, the long, nightmarish journey of a Kurdish family from their homeland in Turkey to reach their paradise in Switzerland. Any hope these refugees may have once harbored gives way to the realities of unscrupulous profiteers and the frozen Alpine mountains. Similarly, in the German film *Dragon Chow*, the hopes of the amiable Pakistani hero and his Chinese business partner to make a life for themselves in Germany prove heartbreakingly naive. In opening their own restaurant, they solve one seemingly insurmountable problem after another, but they are still thwarted in the end and left with nothing.

The So-Called First and Third Worlds

A different type of wall, primarily defined by economics, exists for people who think in terms of First and Third worlds. Whatever the terminology one might use—developed vs. developing, modern vs. primitive, or advanced vs. backward—dividing the world up into these gross blocks leads to false notions of superiority and inferiority as well as to many other misunderstandings.

For American students, the myth to be dispelled is that of a one-sided relationship: Americans give and others take, Americans teach and others learn. The very idea that Third World countries should or would want to develop toward goals defined by others, that they should be provided technical or monetary assistance for the sake of progressing in a direction determined from the outside, seems the epitome of ethnocentrism. The model of linear development itself, with some countries perceived as ahead of others, needs to be replaced by a model of mutual respect, learning, and assistance.

As you address these questions with your students, you will find a wide variety of development films at your disposal. Many of these are produced by international organizations such as UNICEF, the World Health Organization, and the World Bank. They vary widely in quality and run the risk of reflecting the need of the particular organization to demonstrate its success in implementing specific projects. In any case, the point of view presented is usually that of the developer rather than that of those undergoing development. Increasingly, however, Third World filmmakers are finding the means to express their own truths in indigenous cinematic works.

An excellent introduction to the genre of development films is Jean Marie Ackermann's two-volume *Films of a Changing World: A Critical International Guide*. The first volume in particular, taken from Ackermann's critiques as media editor of the *International Development Review* from 1963-71, is not only enlightening, but highly enjoyable. Though many of the films she discusses are currently unavailable or difficult to locate, her unfailing good judgment and easy wit make the reviews valuable reading. The disappointment she expresses, for example, in "Six Development Films: Missed Chances and New Hopes," applies not only to the six films at hand, but to many others of the genre. As she says:

> Films about development tend to stress the final
> product, be it dam or workshop or village well,
> minimizing both the difficulties inherent in its
> achievement and its perspective against the on-
> going culture. This is too bad, and such half-
> truths do disservice to the devoted workers in all
> countries who inescapably know the daily frus-
> tration, apathy, and misunderstandings, as well
> as the exaltation, of successful programs.[6]

Similarly, in a later review Ackermann expresses her feeling, after nine years as a reviewer, that "most filmmakers do not comprehend development, or have the patience to tease out its dynamics." Considering that development of people and places is "the stuff of drama," she is dismayed that so few development documentaries "capture a sense of conflict, striving, excitement, or change."[7]

Since, as mentioned above, many of the films Ackermann reviews are not readily available, a more accessible source is the new film/video collection on Third World Development offered by the Indiana University Center for Media and Teaching Resources in cooperation with the National Film Board of Canada. The collection includes over twenty titles, ranging from *Black Sugar*, which documents the exploitation of Haitian sugarcane workers by growers in the Dominican Republic, to *Solutions and People*, which shows how health workers and technicians in five countries must gain the full support and cooperation of villagers to ensure the success of sanitation and water-supply projects. In Malawi, for example, experts do not attempt to impose solutions from the outside, but are trained to cooperate at every step with the people affected. This means that the engineers locate the probable sites of underground water, but the villagers establish pipe networks according to tribal, clan, and village boundaries, and they also determine the precise location of each well according to their traditions.

Films such as *Solutions and People* lead directly into the ethics and controversies of development. Anyone who watches this film will begin to question the process by which foreign and development aid—whether government or private—is administered. Is it the role of industrialized nations to help other countries become more like us? How can outsiders ever understand the complexities of another culture sufficiently to advocate specific changes? When development aid is provided, are the local people full and willing partners in the effort? How can one be assured that one's assistance, however well-meaning, is truly desired and beneficial?

In the final review of her two-volume work, entitled "Films That Ask," Jean Ackermann says that "criticism, protesting, and asking are part of the sweet music, whether raucous or mild, of free men

reacting to what's happening to them." The good films, she believes, are the ones that "ask, not tell."[8] One such film is the
splendid ten-part series entitled *Millenium: Tribal Wisdom and the
Modern World.* This series discards old models of development in
favor of intriguing questions about what the modern world can
learn from tribal cultures. Anthropologist and narrator David
Maybury-Lewis says that the series is trying to "capture the wisdom
of tribal peoples before it is all gone, before they are all gone."
Maybury-Lewis avoids the tradition of ethnographic films in which
exotic peoples are talked about, explained, and put on display.
Rather, individuals from eleven tribal cultures speak for themselves
and tell their own stories, personal tales that help us to know them
and create links between them and us.

The series is arranged not by portraying one indigenous culture
after another but thematically, with topics ranging from "An
Ecology of Mind" to "The Art of Living." By seeing how individuals
in the various societies deal with existential questions of love and
marriage, poverty and wealth, identity and spirituality, art and
nature, the viewer begins to realize that the choices of the modern
world are not the only viable possibilites. As Maybury-Lewis
explains, "We wanted viewers to meet people who had made different
choices, gone down roads that we ourselves have not taken, but [who]
were confident—and even eloquent—about their own lives."[9] Indeed,
the people in this series speak with sensitivity, thoughtfulness, and
dignity. The choices they are making about their lives may be very
different from our own—such as the practice of polyandry among the
Nyinba of northern Nepal—yet they have their own integrity,
their own purpose. Particularly in light of the urgent problems facing
modern technological society, values that connect people to each
other and to the earth seem to have much to offer.

If you have time to show only one or two of the episodes, you
might wish to use the first, *The Shock of the Other,* which provides
fascinating insights into what it means to encounter people who are
very different from oneself. Maybury-Lewis's reunion after thirty
years with his "brother," Sibupa, of the Xavante of western Brazil,
is a moving example of "the other and the other," meeting from

opposite ends of the world in friendship. The episode entitled *An Ecology of Mind,* which shows the nomadic Gabra of northern Kenya to be consummate environmentalists, is also interesting and timely. In this barren homeland, daily survival depends on intimate knowledge of the desert and a highly regulated way of life. Finally, the episode *A Poor Man Shames Us All* is a fascinating look at wealth in terms of human ties rather than material possessions.

All of the encounters in *Millenium* cause us to raise questions about our own lives, our own choices. From Maybury-Lewis's perspective, the differences between cultures can be a source of renewal, of mutual learning, of inspiration. Yet finding access to each other is a fragile matter, at times even impossible, as poignantly demonstrated in the first episode, in which the entire film crew—after extensive, difficult preparations—is foiled in its attempt to meet with the Mashco-Piro of southeastern Peru. Denied permission to approach a tribe that flees contact with outsiders, the crew has to settle for viewing Mashco-Piro women from afar. But this failure is perhaps also the greatest accomplishment of Maybury-Lewis and his team, for they recognize that walls cannot be stormed, but only crossed when both sides are ready.

Tips for Use: *Millenium*

Would you like to visit any of the groups portrayed in the film series? Why or why not?

Imagine that you could spend an afternoon with Sibupa of the Xavante people in western Brazil. What would you most like to ask him and have him show you? Or, imagine that Sibupa is visiting your town or city. What would you most like to show him?

Write to the organization Cultural Survival (53-A Church Street, Cambridge MA 02138), founded by David Maybury-Lewis, to find out more about its work.

Films Discussed

1. **Arab and Jew: Wounded Spirits in a Promised Land** (2 parts), 1989, 120 mins., color, PBS Video.
2. **Black Sugar,** 1987, 58 mins., color, Indiana University Center for Media and Teaching Resources.
3. **The Boat Is Full,** 1981, 104 mins., color, Facets Multimedia Center. (In Swiss-German, German, and French with English subtitles.)
4. **Carved in Silence,** 1988, 45 mins., color, NAATA CrossCurrent Media.
5. **Cry Freedom,** 1987, 157 mins., color.
6. **Dragon Chow,** 1987, 75 mins., color, Facets Multimedia Center. (In German, Urdu, and Mandarin with English subtitles.)
7. **A Dry White Season,** 1989, 107 mins., color.
8. **Journey of Hope,** 1990, 110 mins., color.
9. **Mapantsula,** 1988, 104 mins., color, California Newsreel. (In English, Zulu, Sotho, and Afrikaans with English subtitles.)
10. **Millenium: Tribal Wisdom and the Modern World** (10 parts), 1992, 10 hrs., color, PBS Video.
11. **Solutions and People,** 1985, 26 mins, color, Indiana University Center for Media and Teaching Resources.
12. **Who Gets In?,** 1989, 52 mins., color, Indiana University Center for Media and Teaching Resources.
13. **A World Apart,** 1988, 112 mins., color.

Related Films

1. **About Love, Tokyo**
   1992, 109 mins., color
   The desperate story of a group of Chinese students living in Tokyo sheds light on the circumstances of thousands of Chinese immigrants struggling to find a place for themselves in contemporary Japan. Mandarin and Japanese with English subtitles.

2. Cannibal Tours

1987, 70 mins., color, University of Washington Instructional Media Services (16mm rental only)

Unusual, thought-provoking film about how tourists, who take luxury cruises up to the Sepik River in the jungles of Papua, New Guinea, and the indigenous people react to each other. Poses questions about the nature and purpose of modern tourism.

3. The Go Masters

1982, 123 mins., color

The first cinematic coproduction between the People's Republic of China and Japan, this masterful epic film tells the highly emotional story of two men, both masters of the game of *go* in their respective countries of China and Japan, and the overwhelming historical events that define their lives over three decades. Japanese and Mandarin dialogue with English subtitles.

4. Happy Birthday, Türke!

1992, 110 mins., color

Filmmaker Doris Dörrie takes viewers into the Frankfurt underworld in a suspenseful detective story that simultaneously poses important questions about the lives of Turks in contemporary Germany. German with English subtitles.

5. The Kitchen Toto

1987, 95 mins., color

Young black houseboy (kitchen "toto") in Kenya is caught between his loyalty to the white family he serves and the growing violence of his Kikuyu people seeking independence from colonial rule.

6. Korea: Homes Apart

1991, 55 mins., color, Third World Newsreel

Producer/narrator Christine Choy travels to Korea in search of her own heritage and, at the same time, traces the journey of a Korean American to find his lost sister in North Korea. The film documents in personal terms the pain felt by millions of families separated for almost forty years by the division of Korea into two countries. This was the first independent film crew allowed to film in both North and South Korea.

7. Place of Weeping

1987, 88 mins., color

A determined black woman struggling against apartheid in South Africa must also face the resistance of her own people.

8. Son of the Exile

1990, 100 mins., color

A moving, insightful film about a Chinese graduate of a British university who returns home to her family in Hong Kong, only to quarrel with her mother and feel out of place. Cantonese and Japanese with English subtitles.

9. Zorba the Greek

1964, 142 mins., b/w

Classic film about the improbable friendship between an exuberant Greek wanderer (Anthony Quinn) and a stuffy British engineer (Alan Bates). Joining as partners in a business venture on the island of Crete, the two outsiders are drawn into the drama of village life. Jean Ackermann calls *Zorba* "one of the best development films ever made."

8

In Our Own Backyard: Cultures
within the United States

When most Americans think of encountering other cultures, they automatically assume that travel is involved, that other cultures are in other countries far away. The idea of crossing cultures tends to imply crossing national borders. Often we do not think of the cultural diversity in our own country as noteworthy, as deserving the effort, expense, and dedication which might go into seeking out or studying differences across the globe.

The films discussed in this chapter will help us become more aware of the ethnic and cultural diversity all around us: in our communities, neighborhoods, schools, and places of employment. As we see in film after film, ethnic and cultural groups are usually divided by fear, suspicion, ignorance, misconceptions, hatred, and violence. I have chosen these films in the belief that once prejudice and discrimination—and their consequences—are exposed, we can learn how to overcome them more effectively. While none of the films actually depicts groups from different ethnic or racial backgrounds living together harmoniously, they all seem to have been created with that vision in mind.

Racism in Our Society

The four documentaries discussed in this section deal not only with racial harassment and violence, but with the refusal on the part of white society to recognize its racism. The first of the four, a 1988 PBS *Frontline* production entitled *Racism 101*, is a disturbing look at the racial attitudes of today's college students. As the first to benefit from school desegregation and other civil rights legislation, this is a generation on which many hopes have rested. Standing at the Lincoln Memorial to recall Martin Luther King's famous speech of twenty-five years past, reporter Judy Woodruff introduces the documentary by asking if school desegregation has fulfilled its purpose of giving "black and white children real contact with each other." Are black and white young adults learning to live together, or, as Woodruff asks, "Is the new generation of students holding on to yesterday's biases?"

Racism 101 focuses on racial strife plaguing three different university campuses. The film is probably most effective when shown in its entirety, but you can use as a separate case study any one of the three incidents examined. The University of Michigan case in particular raises provocative questions about racism in our society. As presented in the documentary, the Ann Arbor campus is torn by racial conflict in the spring of 1987, following a student radio broadcast in which a caller told several degrading jokes about blacks. In protest against this and other indignities, black students in BAM call in Jesse Jackson to help negotiate a series of demands presented to the university. This move produces several concessions on the part of the administration, including a black enrollment target of 12 percent and special pay incentives for black faculty. But in follow-up investigations six months after the Jackson visit, *Frontline* determines that little progress in race relations seems to have been made. After the administration's rejection of a request by student activists to have classes canceled on Martin Luther King's birthday in order to hold workshops, an attempt to stage a collegewide boycott of classes in protest goes largely unsupported by the white majority.

Furthermore, as evidenced by Greek Week in March 1988, socializing obviously takes place in segregated worlds. There are no black members of Steve Kushner's fraternity, and, as he readily admits, he "wouldn't even know where black people hang out." The black fraternities at the university choose not to take part in Greek Week, since they have their own traditions and rituals. As one student explains, "This is a campus of segregation for the most part...segregation by choice." John Sims, a black student who "travels in both worlds" as a member of an otherwise white fraternity, receives a flyer with a poem threatening his safety. The case, referred to the FBI, remains unsolved at the time of filming. Sims admits that by assimilating he is seen as violating the faith of many of his fellow black students.

The film's strength is in allowing students on both sides to voice their personal views, fears, and frustrations. David Colbert explains how difficult it is to relate to white students, whom he perceives as arrogant, and how demeaning it is to be seen by them as a product of affirmative action. "When I walk into a class," he says, "I feel defensive right off the bat." Graduate law student and BAM leader Charles Winder explains why he feels confrontation is necessary for change: "Power doesn't concede anything without a demand."

Several of the white students interviewed seem unable to relate to the situation and concerns of the blacks. Kushner does not see the reason for BAM's demands, since in his view blacks are already receiving equal opportunity. "They're no longer second-class citizens," he says. Another student reacts negatively to a BAM rally, in which the slogan "By any means necessary" is written on various placards: "I definitely felt threatened," he says. "I didn't feel very comfortable." By contrast, Michael Epstein, a thoughtful student who considers both sides of the issue, voices a concern that once a crisis passes, white students may not be able to sustain a commitment to combatting racism. Many white students, he observes, are saying, "Enough. I'm sick of racism. We dealt with that six months ago."

The second story, which also could provide an excellent case study, tells of the systematic harassment over a period of years of black Dartmouth College professor William Cole by the *Dartmouth Review*, a student-run conservative paper located in Hanover, New Hampshire, but not subsidized by the college. Racist, defamatory articles directed at Cole and other members of minority groups have created an atmosphere of tension and divisiveness on campus. The case raises questions relating to the controversial issue of hate speech and is an excellent vehicle for examining the issue of First Amendment protection vs. violation of civil rights. Also, students can examine the reactions of Cole, his supporters, and the Dartmouth College community as a whole to think about how one appropriately responds to this type of harassment.

Tips for Use: *Racism 101*

Observe patterns of social interaction in the cafeteria or snack bar on your campus or at your workplace. Who sits with whom? To what extent do people seem to interact across ethnic, racial, and national boundaries? To what extent does there seem to be segregation, whether by choice or otherwise?

To what extent does your campus seem to encourage and promote diversity? Your investigations can include: obtaining statistics on the presence of students and faculty from diverse backgrounds; examining campus literature to see what images are portrayed; obtaining the mission statement, bylaws, affirmative action guidelines, and other pertinent information to determine current policies; interviewing key people to see what philosophy prevails and what actions are being undertaken; and examining academic catalogs for evidence of diversity in curricular offerings.

Obtain recent copies of the *Dartmouth Review* to see how issues of diversity are being presented. Write an editorial expressing your own viewpoints on an issue of interest.

Further Reading

Beyond P.C.: Toward a Politics of Understanding, Patricia Aufderheide, editor (St. Paul, MN: Graywolf Press, 1992).

Many students who watched *Racism 101* in my classes seemed to experience a rude awakening. In follow-up discussions, these students, most of whom are white, expressed shock and dismay; they said they were largely unaware of the problems presented in the film. Quite possibly many of us hold on to myths of college campuses as oases of openness and liberalism, as havens where people of different backgrounds and persuasions can learn about and from each other. The film shows a different reality, not only by presenting the sobering details of racial strife on three campuses, but by pointing out that in recent years the U.S. Justice Department has recorded an alarming number of racial incidents on college campuses, many of them at the nation's elite institutions, including Harvard, Swarthmore, Berkeley, and Columbia.

Since the film confronts students with racism in their own world of the campus, it leads naturally into discussions of what the environment is like at one's own institution. Depending on their cultural background and experiences, the students will inevitably have widely differing opinions of the same events. Follow-up assignments can open students' eyes to a wide range of multicultural issues as they observe and investigate their own setting. Racism which might have gone unseen or unexamined can become visible if the right questions are asked.

Another fascinating study of racism in America is provided in the documentary *Trouble Behind*. This film focuses on the small town of Corbin, Kentucky, the home of Colonel Sanders Kentucky Fried Chicken. A seemingly typical, all-American community, Corbin has an ugly past that only gradually is revealed as the film unfolds. The focus of investigation in the documentary is the absence of blacks in Corbin. When asked why there is not more than one black family in town, white residents claim that blacks have simply chosen to live elsewhere. One resident admits that at one time there was a racial problem in Corbin, concluding that afterwards the blacks "never did choose to come back and be with us any more."

This one-time problem is traced in the first part of the film, which uses oral history and archival photographs to illuminate the 1919 incident. During World War I, approximately two hundred blacks were hired in Corbin to fill railroad jobs. When the whites returned from the war to find their jobs occupied, trouble erupted. On the evening of October 31, the blacks in Corbin were attacked, beaten, and forced out of town in railroad cars headed ninety miles south to Knoxville, Tennessee.

But this is only one part of the story. Why have blacks not returned to Corbin since 1919? For seventy years, they have stayed away, but not simply by preference. The second part of the documentary uncovers the reasons why blacks feel not only unwelcome, but unsafe in Corbin. One man, Jeff Kyle, moved to Corbin in 1982 to play football but says he left when he received death threats. A black man hired as manager of a McDonald's restaurant left Corbin after a cross was reportedly burned in front of his house. Black residents from a nearby city express fear of being in Corbin after dark. Nancy Rankin, from the Kentucky Human Rights Commission, points out that there is still a street in Corbin named Nigger Creek Road, a clear indication of the town's unwillingness to change.

Meanwhile, most of the white residents interviewed continue to deny that there is a problem. The mayor says that in recent years Corbin has not had a problem with ethnic minorities. One resident even denies that the 1919 riot took place. Another says of the riot, "I think that's really behind us." Finally, one resident claims there is no purpose whatsoever in looking at the legacy of the riot. "Exposure is not the way to correct some misdeed that maybe did take place many years ago," he says. In his view, exposure "creates more problems than it solves."

As African-American historian Dr. Robert Harris says, "Corbin is a window through which we can understand racism in the United States." What he means by this statement can make for stimulating class discussion. What in fact can be learned from Corbin? Do students agree that exposure of past injustices creates more problems than it solves? Or does it seem more likely, as Dr. Stephen Ashmann from the Corbin Presbyterian Church believes, that "forgetting just continue[s] the wrong"? To what extent has Corbin succeeded in putting trouble behind?

You might also ask the students to what extent the film may, perhaps inadvertently, reinforce stereotypes of small-town white Southerners. What is this stereotype and who in the film fits it? Are there any Corbin residents who do not fit the stereotype?

Denying racism, this time in the case of a more recent injustice against a Chinese American, is also the subject of the compelling documentary *Who Killed Vincent Chin?* The details of the Vincent Chin case can be briefly summarized: on the evening of June 19, 1982, in Detroit, Michigan, a twenty-seven-year-old engineer was brutally murdered with a baseball bat by Ronald Ebens, an automotive plant supervisor, following a barroom dispute. Apparently mistaking Chin for a Japanese American, Ebens was overheard shouting racial slurs in the bar, insinuating that Chin and others like him were taking away American jobs. In the first of three trials that ensued over a five-year period, Ebens was allowed to plead guilty to manslaughter and given a light sentence with no jail term. An outraged Asian-American community rallied to demand a new trial. At the center of the protest was Vincent's mother, who overcame enormous cultural and linguistic barriers to lead a nationwide campaign for justice for her son. The subsequent federal trial for civil rights violations resulted in a guilty verdict and a twenty-five-year prison sentence, but this ruling was overturned two years later in a new trial ordered by a federal appeals court, and Ebens was allowed to walk free. The film suggests that the reversal was not a result of additional evidence, but of the relocation of the trial to Cincinnati, where jurors were unfamiliar with the context of the crime.

In a search for the truth behind the case of Vincent Chin, Asian-American codirectors Renee Tajima and Christine Choy skillfully approach the subject from many different angles. The film unfolds almost like a detective story, with details and background material emerging a little at a time. There is no narration, but rather the viewer draws conclusions from a montage of impressions, opinions, and eyewitness accounts intermixed with the sights and sounds of Detroit. All of these bits and pieces prove to be part of a murder case which goes well beyond the individuals involved to include the entire society.

A good place to begin discussion is with the question posed in the title: Who killed Vincent Chin? The documentary provides evidence that responsibility for a crime of this nature is far-reaching; Ebens's act of violence took place in an environment of fear, prejudice, and ignorance. Students can find numerous examples in the documentary of the ways in which anti-Japanese sentiment is incited in industry, politics, and the media. The city of Detroit itself, with its auto industry declining in the face of

Japanese imports, almost becomes a player in the crime against Vincent Chin. Finally, the judicial system contributes to the wrongdoing by sending a message that there is virtually no punishment for taking the life of an Asian American.

At the same time that students examine different levels of responsibility, they cannot but be struck by the absolute lack of accountability. Ebens himself is a troubling case in point. He categorically denies any prejudice: "I'm no racist. I've never been a racist." Nor does he seem to accept any blame; the charges, in his view, were fabricated. In extended interviews on film, he never expresses the slightest remorse, concern for the Chin family, or feeling of personal responsibility. His wife reports that on the evening Vincent Chin died, four days after the attack, her husband was out playing baseball with his team. Ebens's friends also seem unwilling to see any crime. They defend him as a decent family man, and we learn that some had even organized a support group. One friend expresses the feeling that the media blew the incident out of proportion. In the end, the views of Ebens, his family, and his friends—views which can hardly be seen as anything but extreme rationalizations, if not outright untruths—are supported by the legal system.

Racism against Asian Americans on a much broader scale is presented in the superb documentary *The Color of Honor: The Japanese-American Soldier in World War II*. Not only does the film shed light on the illegal internment of thousands of innocent Japanese during World War II, which today remains a little-known chapter in American history, but it traces the invaluable contributions of many Japanese to the war effort. Caught between the land of their ancestry and the nation they call home, and faced with agonizing decisions during a time when they and their families were being persecuted by the government they were asked to support, Japanese men are shown to have served the United States with exceptional courage and honor.

Through emotional personal recollections and testimony, combat footage, and dramatic reenactments, the different paths of Japanese soldiers are brought to life. For example, Military Intelligence Service linguists are shown serving on intelligence-gathering and propaganda teams in highly sensitive positions. Though credited with decoding top-secret Japanese military plans and viewed as General MacArthur's secret weapon, these men could not be publicly recognized at the time and today remain unsung heroes. The viewer is also introduced to men who were part of the 442nd Regimental Combat Team, an all-Japanese regiment that liberated Bruyeres, France, and is thought to be the most decorated military unit in U.S. history. A poignant 1984 reunion at Bruyeres reveals the enduring bonds of friendship between French citizens and their Japanese-American liberators.

Produced by independent filmmaker Loni Ding, *The Color of Honor* was screened before Congress as part of debates for reparations for Japanese Americans interned in World War II. Thus it stands as a corrective statement, a challenge not only to stereotypes, but to the silence surrounding the "American-ness" of Japanese. In follow-up discussion, you can talk with students about their own prior knowledge of this part of history. Have they been introduced to either side—the Japanese internment or Japanese military valor—in school? If so, when and where? Students might examine textbooks and history books to see how much of this information is covered. If Japanese Americans are present in the class, they might be willing to help fill in the gaps with personal insights and stories. Also, students might look at the efforts in recent years to provide reparations and redress. What did the 1988 American Civil Liberties Bill provide for? Was it enough? What other types of action have been taken? In Portland, Oregon, for example, students can visit a recently erected memorial to the Japanese-American internment. Is this type of remembrance important? What other types of action might be possible?

The Other America—A Matter of Identity

Two of the films examined in the previous section raise critical questions about the concept of integration and the realities of segregation. In *Racism 101*, many of the students interviewed—

both whites and blacks—are making choices to live, or at least socialize, in segregated worlds. In *Trouble Behind*, many whites choose segregation but deny that they are doing so.

These same questions are seen from an entirely different perspective in the film entitled *Winds of Change*. This enlightening two-part PBS documentary shows how Native Americans are attempting to define their place in this society.

"I never consider myself a citizen of the United States or an American citizen, never," is the startling opening statement made by Audrey Shenandoah, clan mother of the Onondaga Nation in upstate New York. The first hour, entitled *A Matter of Promises* and narrated by Kiowa author N. Scott Momaday, details the struggles of three Indian nations—the Onondaga, Navajo, and Lummi—to maintain their integrity as separate nations within the borders of the United States. They and hundreds of other Indian nations, which still exist against enormous odds, have inherited painful dilemmas as they attempt to defend and define the sovereign status promised to them by treaty.

As the film shows, the three nations differ in their approach and outlook. Should you wish to use only one of the three stories, the most effective is probably that of the Onondaga. These "people of the hills," whose survival is challenged from within and outside their boundaries, are determined to uphold their traditions and resist outside intrusion of what they call the "philosophy of materialism." A matrilineal people in which women are the landowners and membership is based on the clan system, they have no police force, nor do they associate themselves with the Bureau of Indian Affairs. They even issue their own passports.

The case of the Onondaga is bound to shock students who are not aware of the implications of Native Americans' claims to sovereign status. What does it mean, or is it even possible, to be a sovereign nation within the United States? How does the documentary explain the Onondaga's reasons for their separatism? Do the reasons seem valid? In what areas is controversy likely to exist between the U.S. government and the government of the Onondaga

Nation? How far can sovereignty be taken for territories located within the geographical boundaries of the United States?

The Navajo, seen in the second segment, provide an interesting contrast. Occupying a nation the size of Ireland stretching across parts of Arizona, New Mexico, and Utah, the Navajo are shown to be fiercely patriotic to the United States as well as to their own government. They have served well and proudly in the U.S. military, as a visit to the Navajo Veterans' Cemetery demonstrates, but at the same time they resist intervention in their internal affairs. They have their own police force, elected government, and supreme court. Their peacemaker court differs in philosophy from the Anglo-Saxon idea of blind justice; the Navajo allow no rules of evidence, no legal terminology, and no dispassionate judge. They spend countless hours resolving disputes rather than trying to determine right and wrong.

Because the Navajo feel a loyalty to both governments, their case is pehaps less threatening to the establishment than that of the Onondaga. But their choice for both raises equally interesting questions. Can they truly be loyal to both? Where might the conflicts lie? Will their attempt to have, in a sense, dual citizenship, be understood and accepted by the outside society?

The second part of the documentary, entitled *A Matter of Choice*, shows how personal decisions to belong to one nation or both affect people's lives. This hour is narrated by Hattie Kauffman, a Nez Percé Indian and CBS national correspondent, who was born on a reservation in Idaho and lives in New York City. With half of Native Americans now living in cities and more than half having intermarried with other tribes or non-Indians, the choices become a matter of personal identity and national survival.

Much of the documentary takes place in a Hopi mesa village in Arizona, where residents explain their reasons for remaining on, or returning to, the reservation. Pat Ross, who was away for most of her life, always missed the extended family life of the Hopi; for her, the reservation provides, as Kauffman explains, a "powerful sense of place, centered on the spiritual." Ross believes that the young people should experience life on the outside, for only then will they come to know truly and to value what the Hopi stand for. She trusts that eventually they will return.

For those Indians from all nations who decide to live in cities, newly created intertribal traditions and institutions are becoming increasingly important. According to the film, city powwows and parades, as well as language and culture classes for the young in community schools, help urban American Indians "recreate something of the singular spirit of the reservation."

Other excellent documentaries on the contemporary situation of Native Americans include *River People: Behind the Case of David Sohappy* (discussed earlier; see page 73) and *...And Woman Wove It in a Basket...*, winner of the Best Documentary Award at the 1991 Native American Film and Video Festival. While the makers of these documentaries attempt to capture some of the conflicts and decisions facing Native Americans today, feature films with similar contemporary themes are few and far between. Though it hardly seems fair to criticize a film for not being something it wasn't intended to be, the fact remains that, to date, large-scale feature films, including the enormously successful *Dances with Wolves*, tend invariably to be set in the Old West, featuring Indians who have little connection with the present day (see below for a further discussion of *Dances with Wolves*). Director Bruce Beresford's *Black Robe*, which drew considerable criticism from Native-American leaders, reaches even further into history, to a seventeenth-century French missionary's attempt to save souls amidst warring Algonquin and Iroquois tribes in Canada.

According to Michael Smith, director of the American Indian Film Institute in San Francisco and a Sioux born in South Dakota, the better feature films about Indians are not receiving the attention they deserve. A film entitled *Loyalties*, for example, which "showed American Indians with all the little warts...just like everybody else, not like the stoic people Hollywood made us out to be,"[1] played well in Canada, but could not get distribution in the United States. *Powwow Highway* (1989), an offbeat tale of two Indian friends on the road to New Mexico in a dilapidated Buick, generally drew praise from Native Americans but was not a commercial success. The 1992 production *Thunderheart* is a noteworthy exception and demonstrates that a different type of Native-American story—set in recent times and revolving around current issues—can indeed capture a wide audience.

Because of its phenomenal success and the questions it raises, you might wish to discuss with students Kevin Costner's *Dances with Wolves*. In general, the film has received high marks for casting Native Americans and for using the Pawnee and Lakota languages with English subtitles. All of the Indian roles are played by North American Indians, including prominent actors such as Graham Greene as Kicking Bird, Rodney A. Grant as Wind in His Hair, and Floyd Red Crow Westerman as Ten Bears (all three speak Lakota). Both Kevin Costner and Mary McDonnell, the female lead, were given a three-week cram course in Lakota by Doris Leader Charge, a Lakota instructor at Sinte Gleska College on the Rosebud Reservation in South Dakota. Approximately 30 percent of the film is spoken in Lakota or Pawnee with subtitles. With this decision, Costner breaks from the tradition that depicts Native Americans as unintelligent creatures who are good at war whoops but can only utter a few words of broken English.

Costner has also been praised for his attempt to depict Native-American culture with accuracy. The film crew spent about six months in production, much of it for the sake of ensuring authenticity. The costume designer, Elsa Zamparelli, searched the entire country for the 625 bear skins needed for Sioux and Pawnee costumes and enlisted aid from technical adviser Cathy Smith, an expert in nineteenth-century Plains Indians. Leader Charge also served as technical adviser, assisting with matters ranging from proper seating arrangements around a Sioux chief during a village meeting to the correct way to rig tepees, which were built from an authentic blueprint.

Native-American critics of the film do not take issue with these elements, but they question the film's relevance to current social and economic concerns of Native Americans. Aaron Two Elk, Southwest Regional Coordinator of the International Indian Treaty

Council, believes the film "perpetuates a romanticized image of a culture that would take attention away from the needs of native peoples today." Two Elk also sees the potential for films of this nature to exploit the Native-American heritage. "It's a subtle attempt to prostitute the culture for monetary gain,"[2] he says.

Native-American author Michael Dorris writes in a highly critical article for the *New York Times* that *Dances with Wolves* shares with many other films in the same tradition "a subtle or not so subtle message: Indians may be poor, they may at first seem strange or forbidding or primitive, but by golly once you get to know them they have a thing or two to teach us about the Meaning of Life." Dorris admits that the film will undoubtedly create some goodwill toward the Sioux, but in his mind hard questions remain:

> Will this sentiment be practical, translating into public support for Native American religious freedom causes before the Supreme Court, for restoration of Lakota sacred lands (the Black Hills) or water rights, for tribal sovereignty, for providing the money desperately needed by reservation health clinics?...Or will it turn out, once again, that the only good Indians—the only Indians whose causes and needs we can embrace—are lodged safely in the past, wrapped neatly in the blankets of history, magnets for our sympathy because they require nothing of us but tears in a dark theater?[3]

Dorris's views of the film are not, however, held by all Native Americans. At the American Indian Film Festival in San Francisco, *Dances with Wolves* won awards for best picture, best director, and best actor. Furthermore, Kevin Costner was adopted as a brother of Sinte Gleska College in honor of his outstanding representation of the Lakota Sioux Nation (producer Jim Wilson, scriptwriter Michael Blake, and actress Mary McDonnell were similarly honored). Despite these signs of appreciation and recognition from the Native-American community, one doubts that

Dorris's concerns will be fully addressed until Native Americans have the means to act as producers, directors, and writers in large-scale films of their own making.

Odysseys of Our Times: The New Immigrants

Just as the original inhabitants of the land often find themselves at odds with the larger society, so, too, do the most recent immigrants. An unusual, thought-provoking documentary, *Blue Collar and Buddha*, describes tensions in Rockford, Illinois, between longtime residents and the Laotian refugee community settled there. The film begins with a news segment from a local television station reporting that the Lao Buddhist temple in Rockford has been bombed for the second time. The temple, built by the Laotians on a small farmstead in 1981, is a visible symbol of what many local residents, themselves descendants of immigrants from Sweden, Holland, and Belgium, perceive as an intrusion of alien ways. As one person says: "It was real weird for me to see something like a monk."

Interviews with town residents reveal that much of their hostility comes from the fact that Laotians are seen as beneficiaries in a depressed economy. In a local bar, resentments, many seemingly unfounded, are given free expression. One hears that the Laotians "pay no taxes," that "they live like kings here," or that "they're living better, every one of them, than anybody in this bar." One resident asks, "Does anybody ever pay your rent, give you a car for nothing?" In sum, the prevailing attitude seems to be that the Asians are "cleaning up."

From the point of view of the refugees, the reality is quite different. Through hard work and a willingness to accept jobs no one else wants, the refugees see themselves as earning their way. They took jobs, for example, in Rockford's lagging furniture companies and helped revive an industry originally sustained by Swedish immigrant labor. But their work is not seen as a contribution, least of all by the town's Vietnam War veterans. They feel that the Asians are being given opportunities they themselves never had after the war. "Hire a veteran first" should be the rule to follow, they believe.

The invisible background of the Laotians' lives is revealed in small part in statements made by one of the town's Buddhist monks, who speaks about his daily life and role as helper to his people. For the monk and his compatriots, the building of the temple is a milestone in an arduous process of adaptation to a new land, language, and culture. Having raised the money to purchase the land and build the temple—the center of their spiritual and community life—the Laotians see the structure as a symbol of success and hope after many years of desperate circumstances. To have escaped horrors and violence in their home country only to be faced with attacks against their temple in Rockford is a terrible irony.

The film offers no solutions, not even a hint of reconciliation. What remains in the viewer's mind after *Blue Collar and Buddha* is over are the striking visual contrasts—a monk in flowing saffron robes walking across the Illinois fields or sitting at a computer—and the harsh, uncompromising words of the residents in the local bar.

Tips for Use: *Blue Collar and Buddha*

Imagine that you are a refugee from Indochina who has just arrived in your new hometown or city (use your own place of residence). Assume that you are from a preliterate society, that you speak little English, and that you have no transferable skills. What would your initial thoughts and impressions be? How would you begin to meet your basic needs?

Further Reading

Culture Clash, Ellyn Bache (Yarmouth, ME: Intercultural Press, 1989).

Becoming American also focuses on Laotian refugees, the highland tribal people called the Hmong. The primary emphasis here is not, as in *Blue Collar and Buddha*, on the relationship of the refugees to others in the community, but rather on their odyssey. We accompany one family, Hang Sou and eight relatives, on their journey from the Ban Nam Yao Refugee camp in remote northeastern Thailand to a new home in Seattle, Washington. Upon reaching their final destination in Seattle, the family is greeted by other Hmong who have preceded them and who will help them to adjust.

The film takes us through the first nine months of this bewildering and painful adjustment: the confusion at being introduced to stoves, refrigerators, heat, and indoor plumbing in their apartment; the helplessness in the grocery store, where Velveeta cheese is mistaken for soap and packaged goods hide their contents; the struggle as a preliterate people to come to terms with English; the despair at being considered unqualified for employment. Not only must they adjust to the new language and culture, but they face a second, equally radical, adjustment from agricultural to big-city life. One person interviewed believes that "in their hearts, they would like to be in the hills of Laos."

The long journey to become Americans is filled with peril for these refugees. By focusing on one family, *Becoming American* helps the viewer to identify with the plight of people who might otherwise seem distant and removed from our lives.

These two films—*Blue Collar and Buddha* and *Becoming American*—and over thirty others on recent immigrants are available for rental from the University of Minnesota Film and Video Service. You can obtain from the University a useful annotated list entitled "The Refugee Experience."

African-American Directors of the 1990s

While few Native Americans or recent immigrants have had the means to direct their own films, a new generation of African-American directors has come onto the scene with a wide range of exciting and provocative films within a span of just a few years. In 1991 alone, nineteen films by African-American directors were released, more than in the entire decade of the 1980s. No fewer than eight directors, as profiled in the 14 July 1991 cover story of the *New York Times Magazine*, are breaking new ground by asking difficult questions and grappling with controversial issues. They are presenting views of black life in America from the inside, from the perspective of black directors, writers, producers, actors, and even film crews.

The director who has led the way, with his bold approach to racial issues and his remarkable ability to achieve commercial success on limited budgets, is Spike Lee. Of his early films, the one guaranteed to capture students' interest and stimulate intense debate is the 1989 production *Do the Right Thing*. Widely discussed in the media, it has helped to bring topics of black-white relations and racial violence into public discussion.

Set in the Bedford Stuyvesant section of Brooklyn on the hottest day of summer, the film focuses on the mostly black residents' interactions with the Italian-American family that operates Sal's Famous Pizzeria. In the evening before closing time, tensions in the pizzeria, exacerbated by the heat, lead to a fight between Sal and Radio Raheem, a huge black man who goes nowhere without his boom box. The fight spills into the street and ends with Radio Raheem's death at the hands of the police, followed by a community riot during which the pizzeria is burned to the ground.

The film carefully avoids any suggestion of clear right and wrong. Violence breaks out—and escalates to frightening proportions—but it seems that the blame is either nowhere or everywhere. The irony of the title is that it is not at all apparent what the right thing is. Almost all the characters—with the possible exception of Sal's son Pino—are sympathetic despite obvious shortcomings. Even their prejudices seem human and occasionally comical, rather than threatening. But by the end of the film, the ugly, fearful side of prejudice is fully demonstrated.

As warm-up for the film, you might wish to review with students the Howard Beach incident and other related occurrences. As Spike Lee says about his motivation for creating the film, "We're not only talking Howard Beach: It's Eleanor Bumpers, Michael Stewart, Yvonne Smallwood, etc."[4] Students can research the cases of these three people as well as of the others to whom *Do the*

Right Thing is dedicated in the opening credits, to gain perspective into the film's statement against police brutality.

Because of the film's strong emotional impact, you might begin discussion by having students react to its images, using the technique of the "image-sound skim" (see page 33). One of the images to which students might respond is that of firemen turning their water hoses on the people who fail to disperse. For older people or those who have watched documentaries of the civil rights era, these sights bring back strong memories and could almost be mistaken for 1963 in Montgomery. Clearly the director is using them to ask how much progress has really been made in the intervening decades. Whether students make this visual association, however, does seem to depend on their age; in a recent class of mine, albeit a small one, none of the students was familiar with the fire hoses of the civil rights era.

Another visual image students might mention is the Wall of Fame—the portraits of famous Italian Americans in Sal's Pizzeria. You might ask students how they feel about the wall. Do they agree with Buggin' Out, a vocal neighborhood resident, that Sal should also put up portraits of African Americans, or does Sal have a right to decorate his pizzeria as he wishes? This seemingly minor dispute over pictures on a wall is a perfect illustration of conflicts underlying current debates over multiculturalism. As Henry Louis Gates, Jr., says:

> The movie was a plea for multiculturalism. Sal is the man who is the keeper of the Western canon. He's the person who decides who the all-time greatest hits are on the wall. And this becomes the gate to be stormed.[5]

A sound that reverberates in viewers' ears long after the film has ended is the boom box of Radio Raheem. Students might talk about their own reactions to the sounds before looking at what the boom box means to its owner and to the others. What are these sounds all about? What happens in the stereo standoff between Radio Raheem and the Puerto Ricans? Why does Sal react as he does to the boom box? Students might wish to view Radio Raheem and his boom box within the larger context of rap music and recent controversies over rap lyrics.

As part of the image-sound skim, students might also mention the intense colors of the film—oranges and yellows that reinforce the atmosphere of stifling heat. The feeling of heat was of major importance to Spike Lee, who said, "The film has to look hot, too. The audience should feel like it's suffocating." Spike Lee's idea was that "the heat makes everything explosive, including the racial climate of the city."[6] Especially in view of the riots in South Central Los Angeles following the Rodney King verdict, Lee's film seems in retrospect to be a warning and prediction. Why is the atmosphere in the film so charged? What are the underlying reasons for the outpouring of violence which takes place at the end?

The images of the skim lead in different ways into discussions about the reasons for racial prejudice and violence. As you analyze with students the reasons for the violence, you might wish to replay several of the film's scenes. The first scene between Sal and Radio Raheem, which prepares for the later violence, already shows the failure to communicate on both sides. Students might look at the scene from Radio Raheem's point of view, then from Sal's. How do they antagonize each other? How do their words, their facial expressions, their body posture, their tone of voice all contribute to the air of hostility? What might they have done to defuse the situation?

The same questions can be asked about the scene in which violence erupts. What contributes to the tensions? Why do they escalate? How might they have been defused? Recently I attended a seminar in which a police officer spoke of this scene as a perfect example of the difficulties he and his colleagues face on the streets every day. Forced to make split-second decisions about whether a situation is becoming violent, the officers are especially prone to error, he said, if they are dealing with cultures other than their own. This officer observed that Sal never should have taken out the baseball bat, since the exchange up to that point was verbally aggressive but not violent.

A similar point is made in Thomas Kochman's *Black and White Styles in Conflict.* In a key chapter entitled "Fighting Words," Kochman explains that whites consistently misinterpret verbal aggression by blacks. While whites tend to see loud public disputes as a sign that a fight has already begun and that physical violence is imminent, for blacks the "boundary between words and actions is clearly marked." From the blacks' point of view, arguing, even if there are threats and insults, is still not fighting. "Fighting does not begin until someone actually makes a provocative *movement.*"[7] Kochman gives a number of examples, including one in which two faculty members, a black male and a white female, disagree. The black points a finger at the woman and directs angry words at her, but then, upon seeing her frightened look, immediately softens and says, "You don't need to worry; I'm still talking. When I *stop* talking, then you might need to worry."[8]

Students might interpret the baseball bat scene in light of Kochman's arguments. Or they might look at other scenes in the film as examples of what Kochman is saying. The episode in which a white bicyclist steps on Buggin' Out's Air Jordans is an excellent example. For many whites, the confrontation seems threatening and bound to lead to violence. That Buggin' Out is simply venting his anger and not necessarily looking for a fight becomes apparent when the group peacefully disperses.

Though the main plot revolves around black-white relations, the film also includes significant interactions with Korean Americans and Puerto Ricans. White students in my classes expressed surprise at the tensions shown here between the African Americans and members of these other ethnic groups. One student wrote in her journal, "I hadn't stopped to think that there would be such tensions between ethnic groups other than blacks/whites. I thought they would be more understanding towards *each other* because they had experienced discrimination as outsiders." The subplot with the Korean-American shopowners, in particular, takes on a frightening relevance in light of the riots in South Central Los Angeles.

In *Jungle Fever,* Spike Lee continues to challenge his audiences with a frank exploration of interracial romance. As Lee himself says, "It's about the biggest taboo that's still around—interracial sex."[9] The extent to which Lee hits a nerve with this film is evidenced by the press coverage it received, including a *Newsweek* cover story. The film raises a host of critical issues rarely found elsewhere, such as prejudice among blacks against those with darker complexions and the precarious situation of biracials. Both of these topics are aired in a much publicized scene, a candid, hard-hitting rap session in which a group of black women friends express their anger and frustrations about race and sex.

The film is especially remarkable when viewed against the Hollywood tradition of dealing with interracial romance. You might wish to contrast *Jungle Fever* with early films which plead for separatism, the most blatant example being *Birth of a Nation*. A striking contrast is also provided by the 1967 film, *Guess Who's Coming to Dinner*. Though dealing with interracial marriage, the film scrupulously avoids sexuality, allowing only one chaste kiss, seen in a taxi's rearview mirror. The bride-to-be explains to her mother, an apprehensive Katharine Hepburn, that she has not slept with her black fiancé, but only "because he wouldn't let me!" Sidney Poitier's character, a paragon of virtue and candidate for the Nobel Prize, is, according to Henry Louis Gates, Jr., "the perfect un-Negro"; he is "assimilated, desexualized, safe."[10] Not so Wesley Snipes of *Jungle Fever*.

Of other recent films directed by blacks, two are especially appropriate for our purposes, Matty Rich's *Straight Out of Brooklyn* and John Singleton's *Boyz N the Hood*. Both depict black urban life in conflict with white society. Rich tells of the downfall of a family in Brooklyn's Red Hook project, and Singleton focuses on a group of teenagers growing up in a tough neighborhood of South Central Los Angeles. Drugs, crime, unemployment, gang wars, and domestic violence are all part of the characters' daily lives, yet a sense of the need for positive change pervades both films. *Boyz N the Hood*, in particular, is a pacifist film (its final frames read: "Increase the peace") which stresses the importance of education and the need for fathers to be role models.

These films offer a glimpse of urban black life rarely seen by white audiences. Singleton recognizes that his film will not only be new to many whites, but that a fair number of blacks may find it unfamiliar and alienating as well: "Home boys and hip whites will see it and like it, but it will probably make a lot of bourgeois blacks real uncomfortable."[11]

The question is whether these films will actually reach an audience wider than urban blacks. In an interesting article entitled "Hollywood Seeks White Audience for Black Films," Richard Bernstein says that despite extensive publicity given to at least some of the recent films by black directors, "most black films have not successfully crossed over to a white audience." A studio director from Columbia Pictures, which financed *Boyz N the Hood*, told Bernstein on condition of anonymity that the film had played to an audience of 75 percent black viewers. Several incidents of violence outside movie theaters may have discouraged some potential viewers from attending. But Bernstein says some in the film industry believe the problem lies deeper: "The white audience may not be interested in what these young black filmmakers have to say." While there are some exceptions, according to Bernstein, black movies are generally "a hard sell" for white audiences.[12]

As multicultural educators, we can help to introduce this young generation of filmmakers and their productions to our students. The films deserve serious attention and are excellent vehicles for cross-cultural learning.

The Multicultural Workplace

Since the meeting ground for people from different cultures in American society tends to be the work setting, the final section of this chapter deals with diversity in the workplace. Whether employed in a hospital in Minnesota or a bank in New Mexico, people are beginning to understand the importance of cross-cultural skills. Increasingly, these skills are no longer seen as a luxury, but as a necessity of daily life for all workers. Moreover, the workplace offers a unique opportunity for people from different cultural backgrounds to learn about and from each other. Because diversity usually brings with it formidable problems, however, its benefits can easily be overlooked or forgotten. The challenge for all of us is to focus on the benefits of diversity, rather than the difficulties. We can only do so by an ongoing process of education and training, by constantly reviewing and adjusting our own behavior.

A film with a well-deserved reputation as a classic on diversity in the workplace is A *Tale of O*, written and narrated by Rosabeth Moss Kanter. Because it is told in lighthearted fashion, with a well-crafted script and with graphics instead of people, it is able to address very sensitive issues of prejudice and discrimination without causing the usual discomfort attendant upon such topics. The two types of characters—the numerous "Xs" and the scarce "Os"—are never identified with any specific groups, and thus the tale remains unthreatening.

In the first part of the film, Kanter explores the psychology of being the only "O" in a group of "Xs." Because the "O" stands out, it tends to get extra attention. "Xs" notice more about it, remember more about it, talk more about it. Typical comments from "Xs" might be: "I heard they gave that sales job to an 'O,'" or, "I sure hope I don't have to work for one." While some "Xs" might envy "Os" the attention they get, "Os" tend to feel the pressure of constantly performing in the spotlight. "Os" worry that even the smallest mistakes might be noticed and that their failures might hurt the chances of other "Os," since, as they often hear, "You are our test 'O,'" and "If you do well, we might get more 'Os.'" Also, because there are so few "Os," they often get extra jobs to do, being asked, for example, to serve as the "spokes-O" on numerous committees. If they can't keep up with the overload, assumptions are made that "Os" just can't take the heat.

Kanter explains that, given the pressures of being in the spotlight, of serving as the token "O" and of taking on an overload, "Os" tend to make three choices. Some become overachievers, feeling the need to work more, better, and faster than any "X." But not all "Os" can be superstars, so some opt for a different solution: to try to look like an "X." By dressing, talking, and acting like "Xs," some "Os" can survive, though "Xs" don't always accept this behavior from "Os." A third choice is to hide behind an "X," working totally out of sight: "Behind every great 'X' is an 'O.'"

In the second part of the film, Kanter turns to the "Xs" to see what happens to them when an "O" joins their group. She describes the "contrast effect," which means that the presence of an "O" makes the "Xs" more of a group, causing them to minimize their differences and exaggerate their displays of "X" culture. They now talk more loudly and more often about things they have in common with other "Xs," whether it be football or children. Rather than seeking or recognizing commonalities that may exist with the "Os," they tend to close ranks against them.

Faced with being on the outside with no one to support, recommend, sponsor, or teach them, "Os" usually end up being either good "Os" or bad "Os." The good ones are "not like all those other 'Os'"; they show gratitude for being accepted into the group and may even outdo "Xs" in criticizing other "Os." It would be a compliment for these "Os" to be told that "you think like an 'X.'" Those, however, who speak up or are critical of the organization are soon labeled bad or uppity "Os." They easily become targets for harassment or blame: "It's all because we had to hire 'Os.'" While the good "Os" often receive too much help from patronizing "Xs," the bad ones are given more difficult assignments and more chances to fail. Both types of special treatment—overprotection and over-exposure—are disadvantageous to "Os," since both prevent them from being equal members of the group.

A *Tale of O* is presented in such a way that nearly everyone can identify on some level with the "Os." As Kanter says in the beginning, if you've ever felt different from others around you—whether by reason of race, sex, age, religion, language, size, job specialty, or appearance—you'll be able to relate to the film. A good place to start discussion is to ask people to think about situations in which they have felt like an "O." Depending on the group, it might be better to begin with situations from the past, and later to focus on the current place of employment. What were the circumstances? What happened? What parts of the film did or did not apply?

What can be enlightening for the entire group is the opportunity to hear in how many ways people are routinely excluded from full and equal participation in the workplace. Also, people need to hear from each other about how damaging it is to feel excluded and ostracized. Personalizing the situation of "Os"—with names, faces, and details—can help demonstrate the harm done not only to individuals, but also to the group or organization which alienates or imposes conformity on people.

Exploring the "O" side is only part of the picture. Students should also think about times when they behaved as "Xs," when they purposefully or unintentionally closed ranks against others who were different, gave them too much attention, or forced them to conform. An honest examination of one's own behavior can reveal surprising, and often disturbing, "X" tendencies in all of us.

This short film is so packed with insights, ideas, and provocations that it could prompt hours of reflection and discussion. It is safe enough to use with practically any group as a way of looking at diversity issues in general, but can also be used to help people focus on a specific situation or problem. Whatever the purpose, there should be some attempt to look at solutions, at ways of promoting communication and cooperation between "Xs" and "Os." Again, personal experiences can be shared in an effort to help people approach both "X" and "O" situations in their own lives in new, creative ways.

Produced in 1979, A *Tale of O* was one of the first to address issues of diversity in the workplace. More recently, as organizations across the country—whether in the public or private sector—have recognized the need to provide intercultural training to managers and employees alike, film and video series such as Griggs Productions' seven-part *Valuing Diversity* have been developed. These films can be used effectively in any organization seeking to create a more positive work environment for employees of diverse cultural backgrounds.

Tips for Use: A *Tale of* O
In groups of two, first describe to each other a specific situation when you felt like an outsider. Then describe the emotions involved.
Repeat the exercise, but this time think of a specific situation when you felt like an insider. Describe the situation and, then, the emotions involved.

Since the seven *Valuing Diversity* tapes are geared to different audiences and assume different levels of sophistication from the viewer, they should be selected and sequenced carefully.[13] Part 3, *Communicating across Cultures*, is appropriate for any audience and can be used alone or as the first of several tapes. Like other Griggs Productions tapes, it successfully uses short vignettes, or dramas, to demonstrate the types of misunderstandings that occur between people of different cultures. Rather than merely having experts expound and advise, a failing of many such instructional videos, these tapes bring intercultural theory alive through the dramas, all of which are based on real-life occurrences.

The first video in the *Valuing Diversity* series, entitled *Managing Differences*, demonstrates in five vivid scenes the need for managers and supervisors to make changes both personally and within their organizations to respond to the diverse needs of the work force. Having been taught and encouraged over a lifetime to treat everyone in the same way—to train, motivate, evaluate, and reward uniformly—managers must now learn to understand and respect differences of race, gender, physical abilities, age, ethnicity, culture, and sexual orientation. As Gerald Adolph, Management Consultant from Booz Allen and Hamilton, says, "The fact that we are equal does not mean that we are the same." The five vignettes illustrate how managers in primarily white corporate male settings can begin to share membership more fully with those different from themselves.

For those who have a stake in keeping the organization the way it is, or who are unfamiliar with the ideas presented in *Managing*

Differences, the film can be alienating and threatening. Thus, you should introduce this film only after careful warm-up, and perhaps after first showing Part 6 in the series, entitled *Champions of Diversity*, in which senior executives share their views on the benefits of diversity. A recommended sequence for senior managers is to show *Champions of Diversity*, *Communicating across Cultures*, and then *Managing Differences*.

Other films in the series include *Supervising Differences* (Part 5), intended for first-line supervisors and plant managers; *Diversity at Work* (Part 2), geared to matters of concern to midlevel employees; and *You Make the Difference* (Part 4), dealing with issues involving entry-level employees.

Valuing Diversity is a useful tool in a wide range of settings. While designed primarily for the business world, it will stimulate thought and discussion in any work environment as well as in academic classrooms. Each of the seven films is accompanied by a guide which includes a transcript of the film, extensive background material, a useful bibliography of additional readings, and excellent suggestions for warm-up and follow-up activities. Workshops are also available through Griggs Productions for those who desire training in using the series, and representatives from the firm routinely spend time providing advice and ideas to clients who purchase the films.

Films Discussed

1. **...And Woman Wove It in a Basket...**, 1989, 70 mins., color, Women Make Movies.
2. **Becoming American,** 1983, 59 mins., color, New Day Films.
3. **Birth of a Nation,** 1915, 168 mins., b/w, Pyramid Film and Video.
4. **Black Robe,** 1991, 110 mins., color.
5. **Blue Collar and Buddha,** 1989, 57 mins., color, Filmakers Library.
6. **Boyz N the Hood,** 1991, 107 mins., color.

7. **The Color of Honor,** 1988, 90 mins., color, NAATA CrossCurrent Media.
8. **Dances with Wolves,** 1990, 181 mins., color.
9. **Do the Right Thing,** 1989, 120 mins., color.
10. **Guess Who's Coming to Dinner,** 1967, 108 mins., color.
11. **Jungle Fever,** 1991, 132 mins., color.
12. **Powwow Highway,** 1989, 90 mins, color.
13. **Racism 101,** 1988, 57 mins., color, PBS Video.
14. **Straight Out of Brooklyn,** 1991, 91 mins., color.
15. **A Tale of O,** 1979, 18 mins., b/w, Films, Inc. (rental University of Illinois Film/Viedo Center).
16. **Thunderheart,** 1992, 118 mins., color.
17. **Trouble Behind,** 1990, 56 mins., color, California Newsreel.
18. **Valuing Diversity** (seven parts), color, Griggs Productions, Inc.
19. **Who Killed Vincent Chin?,** 1988, 82 mins., color, Filmakers Library.
20. **Winds of Change** (two parts), 1990, 120 mins., color, PBS Video.

Related Films

1. **Alamo Bay**
   1985, 110 mins, color
   Director Louis Malle bases his story of a small Texas fishing town on the historical confrontation between Galveston Bay shrimp fishermen and competing Vietnamese immigrants. The protagonist, a recently arrived Vietnamese refugee, refuses to yield to intimidation by a resentful Vietnam veteran who ultimately collaborates with the Ku Klux Klan.

2. **American Chinatown**
   1982, 30 mins., color, UCEMC
   Presents intriguing controversy surrounding America's last rural Chinatown, the small town of Locke near Sacramento. This community of sixty elderly, mostly retired Chinese men

has become a curiosity and tourist attraction for people from around the world and has been placed on the National Register of Historic Places. The film asks if this attention is to be seen as a noteworthy preservation of an ethnic landmark or as further manipulation of a long-exploited group of people. More importantly, who should decide on Locke's future? Have the Chinese men themselves been adequately consulted? Excellent reading supplement accompanies film.

3. **Bridges**
   8-part series, color, BNA Communications, Inc.
   Explores, through dramatic scenes, issues critical to managing a diverse work force. Topics include subtle racial stereotypes, cultural "in" groups and "out" groups, communication barriers, and others. Comprehensive trainer's manual included.

4. **Cambodian Donut Dreams**
   1990, 27 mins., color, First Run/Icarus Films
   Ten years after experiencing the horrors of the Khmer Rouge in Cambodia, three immigrants to Los Angeles are making new lives as owners of donut shops. They struggle not only with memories of the past, but with the everyday problems of operating a business in a new culture.

5. **Come See the Paradise**
   1990, 138 mins., color
   Love story of a white union organizer who is separated from his Japanese-American wife and small daughter when the Japanese are sent to internment camps after the bombing of Pearl Harbor.

6. **Eyes on the Prize: America's Civil Rights Years**
   1986, 6-part series (60 mins. each), color, PBS Video
   The story of the civil rights struggle in America between 1954 and 1965 comes alive through news footage, photographs, and personal recollections. Winner of dozens of national awards.

7. **Eyes on the Prize II: America at the Racial Crossroads**
1989, 8-part series (60 mins. each), color, PBS Video
This continuation of the first series traces the civil rights movement from 1965 to 1985.

8. **Glory**
1989, 122 mins., color
Unforgettable epic film about the little-known 54th Regiment of Massachusetts' Voluntary Infantry, an all-black unit that served heroically during the Civil War.

9. **Living on Tokyo Time**
1987, 85 mins., color
Romantic comedy about a young Japanese woman who, in order to stay in the U.S., marries a Japanese-American rock guitarist with no discernible personality.

10. **Miles of Smiles: Years of Struggle**
1982, 59 mins., color, California Newsreel (rental UCEMC)
Extraordinary, largely untold story of the struggle to establish the first black trade union —the Brotherhood of Sleeping Car Porters. Fascinating reminiscences of six retired porters and equally captivating narration by 100-year-old Rosina Tucker, a union organizer and porter's widow. Recovers a period of history significant in itself and as a source of the 1960s civil rights movement.

11. **Mississippi Masala**
1992, 118 mins., color
Directed by Indian American Mira Nair, the film mixes cultures ("masala" is an Indian word for a mixture of hot spices of different colors) by bringing an Indian family expelled from Uganda in the early 1970s by Idi Amin to a new life in Mississippi. Having known and trusted black Africans as a small girl in Uganda, 23-year-old Mina now falls in love with an African American man. Combination of Indian heritage,

African memories, and American daily life make for an unusual, thought-provoking film.

12. **Mosaic Workplace**
10-part series, color, Films for the Humanities and Sciences
Addresses difficulties and opportunities presented by a work force that is increasingly becoming a mosaic of colors, traditions, languages, and values. Titles include: *Valuing Diversity, Understanding Our Biases and Assumptions*, and *Successful Strategies for Minorities*.

13. **Mystery Train**
1989, 113 mins., color
Offbeat film tells three different, yet oddly related, stories of foreigners who stay the same night in the same run-down hotel in Memphis, Tennessee. An entertaining look at the U.S. through the eyes of others.

14. **Stand and Deliver**
1987, 105 mins., color
Based on the true story of a Hispanic teacher, Jaime Escalante (played by Edward James Olmos), whose high school math students in the East L.A. barrio achieve national recognition for their performance on the Advanced Placement calculus test.

15. **Thanh's War**
1991, 58 mins., color, UCEMC
Poignant story of Pham Thanh, a Vietnamese, who at twelve survived a grenade attack by Americans that killed his family and left him badly wounded. Rescued and evacuated to the U.S. for medical treatment, Thanh has now made a successful life in a country he once considered his enemy. Having become an American, he nonetheless maintains strong ties to his homeland, and he must try to reconcile these two cultures within himself.

16. **The Two Worlds of Angelita**
    1983, 73 mins., color, First Run/Icarus Films
    Story of a Puerto Rican family's move from a small town on the island to a barrio in New York's Lower East Side, as seen through the eyes of the nine-year-old daughter, Angelita. Spanish with English subtitles.

17. **Witness**
    1985, 112 mins., color
    Cultures come into conflict when a Philadelphia policeman's only witness to a murder is a young Amish boy.

18. **Zoot Suit**
    1981, 103 mins., color
    This filmed version of Luis Valdez's play deals with the arrest of Chicano gang members for the murder of a young boy in Los Angeles in 1942.

9

Studying and Working Abroad: Tales of Adaptation

It seems safe to say that never in human history have there been so many people on the move—traveling, living, studying, and working in foreign countries. As our technology provides us with the ability to enter and exit cultures—however distant or remote—with ease and rapidity, intriguing questions arise about our psychological and emotional readiness. In the age of jet travel, how are people faring with the transitions they are making from one culture to the other? What role can educators play in facilitating the process of cultural adaptation, especially among student and business travelers?

What International Students Say

In the United States today, colleges and universities send approximately 70,000 students abroad and receive over 400,000 international students each year. These numbers are supplemented by high school exchanges and exchanges of international teachers and scholars. In orientation and reentry programs, as well as in ESL and other classes, educators are helping these travelers to gain insights into the process of cross-cultural adjustment and to deal with the realities of life abroad. A number of excellent documentary and feature films can be used in such contexts to illustrate the confusion and frustration, as well as the exhilaration, of encountering a new world.

Among the videos used most frequently on college campuses is *Cold Water*, produced in 1986 at Boston University by Noriko Ogami. The film increases awareness of international student adaptation. Twelve university students from twelve countries are interviewed about their adjustment to U.S. life, with additional commentary provided by one American student and three cross-cultural specialists. The topics are wide-ranging, including first impressions, privacy, time, greetings, and friendship. The students give the impression of fitting more or less into the classic curve of culture shock, with an initial period of disorientation (described by Tina Lang from Germany as a "plunge into cold water") accompanied by all sorts of difficulties. Looking back, David Martin of Indonesia remembers: "I was sort of slowly falling apart." By the end of the year, however, the students reach a new accommodation with their host culture, feeling more comfortable and as if they can handle it.

Cold Water is useful for international students and scholars, but it can also be shown to Americans interested in how others see us. If you use it with Americans, you should be prepared for some unfavorable reactions, or at least some heated discussion. The discussion usually centers not on the criticisms of the U.S. voiced by the international students, but on the judgments expressed by Dr. Robert Kohls, consultant and author of several cross-cultural books. Kohls offers provocative opinions, most of which are highly critical of Americans. He says, for example, that Americans are "very ignorant of the rest of the world" as well as "very ethnocentric and very egocentric." With regard to friendships, Kohls believes that Americans are satisfied with "shallow interactions"; the type of deep and lasting friendship common in many cultures is something that "most Americans don't experience and never will."

If you use *Cold Water*, you will need to see whether this type of provocation proves useful or distracting. Since the film consists totally of interviews and may become somewhat repetitive, you may decide to edit it, preserving some of the more lively, insightful sections. For example, the comments by Kikaya Karubi from Zaire on his experience with an impatient counter employee at Burger King is illuminating, as is his explanation of why he would choose not to show up at a party rather than to decline an invitation.

Tips for Use: Cold Water
What in the film annoyed? Upset? Surprised you?
Interview an international student on your campus about the issues addressed in the film. Or, invite an international student to watch and discuss the film with you.
How might the film influence the ways in which you relate to international students on your campus?
If you were to make your own video on international student adjustment in the United States, what would you do differently from *Cold Water*?

A second video similar to *Cold Water* is *The Dull Guys*, produced by Elena Garate of the University of California under NAFSA's Cooperative Grants Program. The title comes from an opening statement by an international student who says that while half the people on his dorm floor spend their time partying, the dull guys like himself just study. His statement is indicative of the types of conflicts that can arise for international students, who often come to the States with this one serious purpose in mind. Some of the most troubling problems they face have to do with roommates. Take, for example, the case of an Asian student who does not know how to deal with the fact that her American roommate invites her boyfriend to sleep over. Another hazardous area for international students is that of learning how to choose the right classes from among the overwhelming options. Finally, the video shows some of the frustrations international students face while learning to function within the university bureaucracy.

Though the video tackles some sensitive areas, such as that of offensive cooking and body odors, it does so carefully and thoughtfully. It can be used as a springboard for conversation, not only among international students, but among residence hall staff, American roommates, and university personnel.

In addition to *The Dull Guys*, NAFSA: Association of International Educators makes available a number of other videotapes intended to facilitate the adjustment of international students and scholars. These films serve as useful resources, despite the fact that they lack the polish of commercial productions, since most of them were made by university staffs on limited budgets. Specific topics include how to take safety precautions in big cities (*A Little Street Wisdom*), sexual harassment of international students (*The Wrong Idea*), locating and securing housing (*Where Will I Live?*), achieving success as a graduate student (*What Is Expected of Foreign Graduate Students in the U.S.?*), and meeting the challenge of being an international student spouse (*The Way We Are Living Now: Portraits of International Student Spouses*).

Americans Abroad

The finest videotapes for the American business traveler are produced by Griggs Productions in a seven-part series entitled *Going International*. The first two tapes in particular serve as excellent introductions to cross-cultural issues not only for businesspeople, but for anyone planning international study, work, or travel.

The first tape, *Bridging the Culture Gap*, is a concise, colorful explanation of what culture is and how it affects our lives. What could easily be a boring lesson is instead a lively, intelligent glimpse into the profoundly different ways in which people from various cultures approach life. The film touches upon many important areas—greetings, dress, food, cleanliness, language, relationship with nature, and views of time and space—and gives in just a half hour an overview of how culture influences everything people do. Striking, interesting visuals from various countries around the world are accompanied by excellent commentary from both intercultural experts and international business executives.

I have used *Bridging the Culture Gap* for a number of years with very good success in study-abroad orientations as well as in classes. It provides a solid basis for cross-cultural study, introducing not only basic concepts, such as stereotyping, but also more sophisticated notions, such as the contrast between the directness of Americans in conversation and the more indirect approach of Saudi Arabians.

The second video, *Managing the Overseas Assignment*, is intended to accompany the first and can easily serve as a continuation of its themes. Vignettes set in five different countries—Japan, Saudi Arabia, England, India, and Mexico—all feature rather uninformed, insensitive American businesspeople who blunder badly, alienating the host nationals. In each case, the offender's behavior is analyzed, often by the same commentators as in the first film.

The dramas each demonstrate different insights into intercultural interaction. The vignette set in Mexico, for example, shows how in some cultures interpersonal relations must precede business. The scene opens in a lovely outdoor restaurant, where a seated American, Mr. Thompson, waits impatiently for his Mexican counterpart to arrive. When Mr. Herrera finally comes, Thompson is eager to present his line of new equipment. Despite repeated signals from Herrera that the business can wait while the two men enjoy a brandy, the meal, the guitar music, and even a tour of the local sights and the beautiful National Cathedral, Mr. Thompson remains single-minded, to the point of parody. As Mr. Herrera later explains in an interview, he felt that Thompson was talking not to his host, but only to himself, or even to his catalogs. Commentator Fanchon Silberstein from the U.S. Department of State remarks that by paying attention to the National Cathedral and getting excited about it, the American could have made "great strides" toward the final negotiation, much faster in any case than by "pushing the contract."

The video's five scenes serve to make people aware that their behavior and actions may have unexpected consequences, that what may be normal, acceptable behavior at home may have abysmal effects abroad. This alone is an eye-opener for many people and serves a valuable purpose in causing them to think about how they might offend or be misunderstood. The danger, however, which I have observed among students, is that the video can arouse unnecessary fears. Some students, particularly those with no international experience, seemed quite upset and worried after watching the video, feeling perhaps that they, too, would be candidates for such naive errors. Thus I have found it important in follow-up discussions to talk about mistakes and how to correct or, even better, avoid them.

One question which usually elicits thoughtful discussion is why the five Americans commit so many blunders. In a recent class, a student said she was especially disturbed by the mistakes made by Mr. Wilson, who insults his Saudi hosts by showing the soles of his feet, refusing coffee offered in hospitality, and using his left hand. The student felt she would have made the same mistakes, knowing little about Saudi culture. Another student, however, pointed out that any responsible person doing business in Saudi Arabia would prepare enough to know at least these basics of the culture.

The question then arose as to what to do about the many things for which there is no preparation. Perhaps the most important point demonstrated in all five vignettes is that by reading signals, one can often tell when something is going wrong. In discussing the vignettes with the group you can explore the details of each case, noting how and when the American should have picked up on the signals and changed direction. You might want to replay scenes for the purpose of this more careful analysis.

Another point to emphasize is that the video is showing extreme cases. Students need to know that, in general, people are quite forgiving of a foreigner's mistakes, so long as they feel that the person is sincere and trying not to offend. In the video, the five Americans' fatal flaw is their arrogance, along with a good dose of insensitivity and pushiness. This combination is not likely to create goodwill and tolerance for mistakes.

Depending on the sophistication of the group, you might want to address the ethical question of how far one goes in an attempt not to make mistakes, that is, how far does one adjust to the expectations of another culture before losing one's own integrity? Are there cases where one might deliberately decide to do things one's own way, even if this might not be standard practice elsewhere? For example, if women are expected to behave in a certain way in Saudi Arabia—as American women soldiers indeed found to be the case during the Gulf War—how might one reconcile one's own views with the expectations of the host culture?

Furthermore, you might look at the motivation behind acts of accommodation. Why exactly does one adjust? Is it out of respect for the hosts, or are there other, more self-serving reasons? In these two videos, people clearly are adjusting in order to close business deals. What are the ethics involved here? Silberstein rightly suggests that the American in Mexico would have had more success had he visited the cathedral, but what if he were doing so only as a business strategy? What about Bob Rix, who in the first video concludes his description of the festive meal he attended in Saudi Arabia by saying with slight exasperation that it took him "about nine hours to get a work-hour variance"? Is he an effective executive who knows how to get the job done, or is he manipulating his hosts and taking advantage of their hospitality?

These two videos provide many points of discussion. They are especially useful for people new to international work and travel, but they can also be used with more experienced professionals. If you use them with groups not in international business, you should mention beforehand that while they were made for business, the principles demonstrated apply in other contexts as well (see page 26).

A Case Study: Japanese and Americans

While *Going International* applies to foreign business and travel in general, other videos are available if you wish to focus on a specific country, especially if that country is Japan. As Japan has emerged as a world economic power, presenting Americans with a host of unprecedented difficulties as well as opportunities, filmmakers have engaged a wide spectrum of issues relevant to American-Japanese relations. Thus one finds not only educational films offering practical advice on how to do business successfully in Japan and documentaries on American ventures in Japan, but also comedies about collaboration between such occupational groups as American and Japanese auto workers (see page 15 for a discussion of *Gung Ho*) and rock singers (*Tokyo Pop*). Unfortunately, the relative abundance of films on the U.S./Japanese cultural encounter is not matched by similar resources focusing on interactions between Americans and people from other countries.

The most comprehensive, up-to-date information on video for those wishing to conduct business with the Japanese is the six-part series *Working with Japan*. In the first hour, entitled *Preparation*, emphasis is placed on the need for extensive background work before beginning a new venture or partnership. In Japan, it is explained, things must be done the right way the first time. Narrator Ted Dale says that one cannot simply enter the Japanese market hoping to learn quickly or learn by trial and error, for the first errors may be fatal. According to Dale, the idea that you always have a second chance, or that if things don't work out, you can always move to another place and start over, is very much an American concept that does not hold true in Japan. This view is confirmed by Sheridan Tatsuno, author of *Created in Japan*, who says that while "America is a forgiving society," in Japan mistakes destroy one's credibility. Frank Caffrey, Japan trade specialist from the U.S. Department of Commerce, comments that in Japan, the "first approach should be as perfect as possible."

In the interest of this vital preparation, the first half of the video lays the groundwork for any business dealings in Japan by outlining key cultural differences between Japan and the U.S. These include such areas as personal identification (individual vs. group), social status (egalitarian vs. hierarchical), and communciation (direct vs. indirect). Critical concepts such as *amae*, *on* and *giri*, and *honne* and *tatemae* are explained in clear, understandable fashion.

In a vivid illustration of cultural differences, John Condon, author of *With Respect to the Japanese*,[1] takes the viewer into American and Japanese kindergarten classrooms. Condon's research shows that the same task of drawing one's family not only produces different results in the two countries, but, more importantly, it is undertaken in completely different ways. The Japanese children, for example, tend to confer with and help each other, whereas the American children work on their own. The two groups of four- and five-year-olds already display the same cultural attributes observable in the different styles of Japanese and American business.

Because the first twenty minutes of the video are so filled with information, the producers recommend that the facilitator pause for questions and discussion before proceeding with the second part, which includes practical steps and strategies for success in eight areas ranging from market research and strategic planning to proper introductions and gift giving. A wealth of suggestions and ideas are presented and explained by experienced businesspeople and educators. Again, because the video is packed with information, you will need to stop it or replay sections to allow for discussion, examples, and clarification.

In the second video, an American business team is taken through an initial face-to-face meeting with its Japanese counterpart. David Johnston and John Walters, representatives from a midsized company named NDX, are well informed about appropriate protocol, beginning with introductions, business card exchange, and bows and handshakes. They respect the flow of conversation from general to specific topics, are prepared to present their company background, and are skilled in the use of questions and humor. By watching them interact with their Japanese counterparts and listening to the accompanying commentary, viewers are introduced to a wide range of cultural differences that may affect the success of a first meeting.

The series *Working with Japan*, though intended for Americans doing business in Japan, contains cross-cultural perspectives useful in many settings—Japanese language classes, ESL classes for Japanese students, international business and management classes, and orientation for American students going to Japan.

A concrete example of a company that has achieved the type of success strived for in *Working with Japan* is provided in *The Colonel Comes to Japan*. After asking in the opening narration whether a "gentleman from Kentucky [can] make it in the Land of the Rising Sun," the film shows how Kentucky Fried Chicken has indeed managed to avoid the high failure rate of American businesses in Japan, from the opening of its first restaurant in Japan in 1970 through its growth to more than three hundred fast-food outlets in the next decade. The film credits Kentucky Fried Chicken's success in Japan largely to its ability to adapt to the needs and expectations of a different culture.

Dramatic examples of this adaptation are given throughout the film, beginning with the hiring and training of employees, who expect to be hired for life. Chairman of Kentucky Fried Chicken Japan, Loy Weston, explains that employees do not think of themselves as working for Kentucky Fried Chicken, but rather as belonging to it. Their training can be quite extensive, since the company invests in them as permanent employees, and the company's whole approach to selling is changed to conform to Japanese culture. Modifications affect the size and shape of the stores, which need to be about one-third the size of U.S. stores in a land of costly real estate and narrow streets; the menu (Japanese don't like mashed potatoes and find cole slaw too sweet); the type of marketing and advertising (which focuses on the aristocratic elegance of the food!); and the opening-day celebrations, which include a Shinto ceremony.

Though *The Colonel Comes to Japan* was filmed in 1981, it remains a valuable resource, one of the best of its genre. Prior to viewing, students should know that your purpose is not to give up-to-date *information*, but to provide insight into the types of problems and issues that arise when people attempt to do business in countries and cultures different from their own. This caveat applies to any film about a specific international venture, since even the most recent productions become quickly outdated in a rapidly changing business world. If current information on a particular company or business venture is deemed necessary, it can be provided as a supplement to the video.

As with *The Colonel Comes to Japan*, adapting to the rules of Japanese society is also the theme of the fascinating PBS documentary *American Game: Japanese Rules*. The filmmakers' goal here was to find out how Americans are faring in a society which "plays the game their own way," whether in business or in baseball. Indeed, baseball is the focus of the first segment. The Japanese idea of saving face by playing for ties—or at least by making sure one does not win or lose by too much—is alien to American athletes. Though regarded as celebrities and paid high salaries, the American players are frustrated and perplexed. The most outspoken critic is Steve

Hammond of the Nankai Hawks, who reveals his exasperation at not being allowed to play "the old-fashioned way." He says the way the Japanese play is brutal and stupid. While Hammond is unable to adapt, Leon Lee, a ten-year veteran of Japanese baseball, is more willing to see things from the Japanese point of view. He explains that when the Japanese umpire expands the strike zone on American players, putting them at a distinct disadvantage, this is seen as a fair way to compensate for the size and strength of the Americans.

In a following segment dealing with the rules of the "game" of business, representatives from Corning Glass Works talk about how difficult it is to break in to a market in which price and quality do not so much determine commercial success as do old relationships. Corning executives find that the rules of the marketplace are "different from anything Americans have been taught to believe." The same applies to Don Spiero, owner of Fusion Systems, a successful American company engaged in patent disputes with Mitsubishi. From Spiero's American point of view, the Japanese have simply reverse-engineered his technology and stolen it, threatening the future existence of his firm, but the Mitsubishi executives defend their behavior as completely acceptable within Japanese law.

To find an American living in harmony with Japanese society, the filmmakers leave the metropolitan area for a farm region five hours outside Tokyo. Here a woman named Debby lives with her Japanese husband and two sons, willingly accepting the role expected of her as a Japanese farm wife and becoming completely integrated into village life. Debby has almost entirely abandoned her American ways, for, as she explains, "You cannot take your American views, your American customs, and try to live in Japan." She has adapted so thoroughly to her adopted culture that relatives and neighbors think of her as "almost more Japanese than the Japanese." The segment offers extraordinary testimony to one woman's ability to enter and accept a culture very different from her own.

American Game: Japanese Rules raises fascinating questions about intercultural interactions. Whose rules are to be respected and why? How much accommodating can, or should, be expected of each side? Because Americans tend to believe that their rules are right and will ultimately prevail, the undeniably successful, seemingly uncompromising Japanese way confronts us with a challenging situation. What can Americans learn from dealing with the Japanese, who do not yield to our economic or military strength, who do not seem inclined to come around to doing things our way? In several classes, students were intrigued by the film and willing to respect, at least on an intellectual level, the rules of the Japanese. On an emotional level, however, they admitted that they definitely reacted as Americans. The ball game, they felt, should be more competitive, and the patents were being stolen by Mitsubishi. Students left class concerned about where the common ground and compromises might be between two societies each so committed to its own way.

Tips for Use: *American Game: Japanese Rules*

The American woman Debby, who has lived in Japan most of her adult life, suggests that she might now find it difficult to return to America. What do you think she might find difficult about life in the States?

Have you ever been in a situation in which your rules were not the ones that were generally accepted? Describe the situation and your feelings.

In a group of five or six debate the idea of "playing for ties."

Films Discussed

1. **American Game: Japanese Rules,** 1988, 60 mins., color, PBS Video.
2. **Cold Water,** 1986, 48 mins., color, Intercultural Press, Inc.
3. **The Colonel Comes to Japan,** 1981, 30 mins., Coronet/MTI Film & Video (rental University of Washington Instructional Media Services).
4. **The Dull Guys,** 1986, 30 mins., color, NAFSA.
5. **Going International** (7 parts), 165 mins., color, Griggs Productions, Inc.
6. **Gung Ho,** 1989, 111 mins., color.
7. **Working with Japan** (6 parts), 25-35 mins. each, 1991, color, Intercultural Training Resources, Inc.

Related Films

1. **City of Joy**
   1992, 134 mins., color
   A disillusioned Houston surgeon (played by Patrick Swayze) heads for India in search of spirituality. Though intending to stay away from medicine, he is soon caught up in efforts to assist the desperately poor dwellers of a Calcutta slum called the "city of joy." Some meaningful cross-cultural encounters take place against a backdrop of extraordinary shots of daily life in this tumultuous city.

2. **Cowboy in Mongolia**
   1989, 51 mins., color, First Run/Icarus Films
   Almost twenty years after having fought in the Vietnam War, Oregon rancher Dennis Sheehy achieves his goal of returning to Asia on a peaceful mission. Hired by the Chinese government to help save the grass-covered steppes of Inner Mongolia from further ecological destruction, Sheehy and his family become the first Americans to live among Mongolian herders in remote Yihenoer Sumer.

3. Cultural Diversity: At the Heart of Bull

1982, 28 mins., color, Intercultural Press, Inc.

French and American employees of Bull HN Informational Systems provide a candid view of cultural differences in the workplace. Whether the issue is how brightly lit offices should be, how to structure the workday, or what the manager's role should be, revealing differences in style and philosophy emerge. In English and French with subtitles in both languages.

4. Kyocera Experiment

1982, 30 mins., color, Coronet/MTI Film & Video (rental University of Washington Instructional Media Services).

Candid look at some of the tensions and misunderstandings that arise—especially between Japanese managers and American salespeople—when Japanese owners of the enormously successful Kyocera Company attempt to transplant their management style to the San Diego subsidiary.

5. Local Hero

1983, 111 mins., color

A charming, leisurely film about a Houston oil-company representative sent to buy up a coastal village in Scotland and turn it into a refinery site.

6. One Man's Multinational

1982, 27 mins., color, University of Washington Instructional Media Services

Critical look at the global empire built by Thomas Bata, owner of the world's largest shoe company. Insisting that politics do not concern him, Bata goes wherever he can make shoes at a profit, including countries with dictatorships. Poses important ethical questions for those doing business in today's global marketplace.

7. **A Portable Life**
   1981, 30 mins., color, rental, Syracuse University
   Four women—British, Australian, French Canadian, and English Canadian—who have lived abroad with their husbands for many years in a wide variety of countries speak about the hardships and rewards of a portable life. Useful in helping families prepare to travel abroad and to come back home.

8. **Tokyo Pop**
   1988, 99 mins., color
   New York punk rocker, played by Carrie Hamilton, decides to try to make it big in the musical scene in Japan. When she teams up with a Japanese partner (real-life Japanese rock idol Yutaka Tadokoro), she becomes Japan's hottest new rock star. A charming film with surprising insights into the difficulties of cross-cultural communication.

10

Indeed I Have Hope: Succeeding across Cultures

Many films discussed in the preceding chapters deal with the misunderstandings, conflicts, and animosity caused by cultural differences. At times it almost seems that the distances between people are too great, that change is impossible. The films discussed in this final chapter demonstrate that crossing over not only is possible, but can be enormously rewarding. The people in these films are willing to learn, to change, to take risks. Some dare to believe that barriers of discrimination and inequality can be eradicated, and they are willing to work for reform. Some see difference as a source of enrichment and inspiration, and, in their creativity, they themselves are inspirational. Perhaps most importantly, the people in these films are struggling to tear down the barriers within themselves and learning how to cross borders in their own lives.

Efforts of Individuals

The organization Foundation for Global Community/Beyond War has available two inspiring short tapes that describe the efforts of ordinary people to reduce the enmity between hostile groups. The first, *Indeed I Have Hope*, by Hennie Serfontein, tells how the Koinonia organization in South Africa brings blacks and whites together. The organization's idea is simple but revolutionary: small "meal groups" are established, so that two white couples and two black couples take meals once a month on a rotating basis in each other's homes. A future goal is to go to restaurants, cinema, or church together as a public and visible sign of their bond.

Both blacks and whites speak of the transforming quality of this "first encounter with people of another race on an equal basis." A black participant, Palesa Moruda, says that previously the only white people she saw in her home were the police, who were "very harsh." Ena van der Merwe, a white participant, says that "whites live in fear constantly," without knowing why. Her visits to black homes have eliminated this fear. "You grow out of it," she says. "You're not afraid any more."

Neve Shalom/Wahat al-Salam, the second short tape, is actually a CNN news report that tells of a settlement in Israel where Arabs and Jews live together. Located on a hillside between Jerusalem and Tel Aviv, the settlement is called Neve Shalom in Hebrew and Wahat al-Salam in Arabic, both of which mean "Oasis of Peace." For almost two decades, a group of sixteen Arab and Jewish families have lived and worked there as partners, sharing their everyday lives and dealing with their differences. The children attend a three-room schoolhouse, where classes are taught in both languages; everyone in the settlement speaks the other's language. In interviews, the residents from two families describe themselves as normal people who simply wanted to put their hopes and pains toward something positive.

Because cross-cultural work is often so difficult and discouraging—especially when a long history of animosity and bitterness exists—these two short films are invaluable as glimpses of hope. They show that, against all odds, people can find ways to bridge their differences. The films are especially inspiring in that they focus on the efforts of ordinary people. These people have no particular training, background, or qualifications for what they are doing, nor do they see themselves as special. While harboring no illusions about changing the world overnight, they nevertheless seem to gain strength from doing at least this much. "What we are doing," says Abed Najjar from Wahat al-Salam, is "better than nothing."

As an alternative to borrowing these two tapes, it might be more practical simply to look for similar examples from the news. Just as the above tape on Neve Shalom is actually a CNN report, other examples of success stories are often presented on the news or in documentaries. Another possibility is to use excerpts from longer films; *Arab and Jew* (see page 96), for example, contains several segments similar to the report on Neve Shalom, as does *Talking to the Enemy* (discussed below).

An intense, moving documentary which explores in much greater depth the psychology of crossing over in the same Arab-Israeli context is producer Mira Hamermesh's *Talking to the Enemy: Voices of Rage and Sorrow*. The film traces the friendship between two individuals—a young female Palestinian journalist, Muna Hamzeh, and an older Israeli magazine editor, Chaim Shur—from their first meeting in Washington, D.C., in 1985 to her eventual acceptance several years later of the invitation to visit his kibbutz. Their relationship is seen against the background of Arab-Israeli hostilities, and their story is beautifully interwoven with other stories of their two peoples.

Hamzeh, we learn, was born in East Jerusalem but is living in Washington and longs for her homeland. For a period of years she was active in student circles in the U.S., making, in Chaim Shur's words, "fiery speeches against the Zionists." In her Washington apartment, she prominently displays a picture of Yasir Arafat shaking her hand, and she wears a necklace in the shape of Israel with the word "Palestine" written across it.

In a parallel account, we learn that Shur, editor of the *New Outlook* magazine, is willing to share the land of Israel with the Palestinians. This conciliatory stance is not popular among fellow Israelis, as evidenced by the threatening mail received by Shur and his colleagues on the magazine staff. Shur invites Hamzeh to visit him in an attempt to open genuine dialogue, but she is reluctant: "It's just not something that you do, that you just walk over to the enemy, and talk to him or her, and visit them, and be in their homes." Accepting the invitation seems impossible, not only because of her own politics, but because she fears that other Palestinians will disapprove: "I was afraid that it was going to isolate me, that my people would misunderstand it."

Finally overcoming her fears and uncertainty, Hamzeh travels to Israel to spend time with Shur and, ultimately, with his family on the kibbutz. The final scene of Hamzeh at Shur's home, with his wife and son, is among the most powerful examples in film of the emotional cost of trying to make peace with one's enemy. What the four people talk about is so painful as to be almost unbearable. As years of suffering and anguish surface on both sides, there is disagreement and tension, but there is also affection. It becomes evident that there are no immediate solutions and no clear signs of hope, other than the fact that both sides display the will to continue talking. At the end Hamzeh says that she never in her entire life imagined she would be on a kibbutz in the middle of Israel, for that would be the "ultimate sin"; but she now calls it a privilege not only to have crossed over, but "all the way to the other side."

As the Shur/Hamzeh story is being told, a number of fascinating scenes, interspersed throughout the film, illuminate the background of the conflict dividing them. Especially telling are two discussions among Jewish women at the Feminist Centre in Tel Aviv, as they struggle with the question of how to create a dialogue with Arab women. One woman says, "Since we are not the underdog, it's our job to really reach out to them." But another sees survival of the Jewish people as the top priority: "One day we will be able to create a dialogue, but not yet."

Another *Talking to the Enemy* scene worth replaying and analyzing in detail with students is the one showing Yoram Binur, an Israeli journalist, who disguises himself as an Arab to see how the Palestinians are being treated. In a Jewish neighborhood, Binur first sits down on a park bench next to a woman eating a sandwich. Binur has hardly opened his magazine when the woman, sandwich only half eaten, gets up and walks off. The scenario repeats itself with an elderly gentleman on a park bench, whom Binur frightens off simply by asking him something. In a third situation, Binur enters a café in Jerusalem and sits down at a table. He feels not only conspicuous and unwelcome, but realizes that he is feared. He says that everyone was looking at a bag he was carrying as if he were going to blow up the café. "An Arab is like a walking bomb," he realizes.

You might examine with students what it is exactly that the Jews seem to be reacting to. Does Binur give off threatening signals? Does he do anything wrong? Is it simply his appearance? You might also look carefully at how the two people on the park bench behave. Do they appear to be uncomfortable? Worried? Are they rude? The scene powerfully reveals the extent of the antipathy and alienation between the two groups, to the point of total avoidance. A question you might explore further is what an exercise like Binur's accomplishes. What can one learn from his tactic?

The Binur segment makes the interaction between the Shur family and Hamzeh all the more remarkable. You can analyze with students both the personal and political hindrances to such a friendship and the breakthroughs achieved by it. What makes the dialogue possible despite all odds? What is it that creates the bond?

Tips for Use: *Talking to the Enemy*

Have you ever regarded a person or group as an enemy? Have you ever been seen as an enemy by others? What do you think caused this type of thinking?

Think of a time when you had an intense conflict with a person or a group. Was the conflict resolved? If so, what made the resolution possible? If not, what do you think were the main barriers?

What peace groups are active in your area? Contact several of these groups to see what type of work they are doing and how interested members of your class might become involved. Collect their literature to distribute to the class and inquire as to the availability of representatives who might speak to the group.

Further Reading

Arab and Jew: Wounded Spirits in a Promised Land, David K. Shipler (New York: Penguin, 1987).

My Enemy, My Self, Yoram Binur (New York: Doubleday, 1989).

A final example of the efforts of two individuals to cross the seemingly fixed boundary between them is provided in the dramatic feature film *The Long Walk Home*, a scene from which was examined earlier for its depiction of failed communication (see page 91). As in *Talking to the Enemy*, this film explores the psychology of moving toward each other, of refusing to accept the dictates of a society that separates people. The two main characters, Odessa Cotter, a black domestic, and Miriam Thompson, for whom she works, undergo a transformation in their lives and their relationship to each other. The changes are initiated by Cotter, a woman who finds the strength and courage to move in a new direction. That she belongs in the center of the story is recognized by Mary Catherine, the Thompsons' daughter, who narrates as she looks back at the events of her childhood. In the opening lines of the film, she says of Odessa, "There wasn't anything extraordinary about her...but I guess there's always something extraordinary about someone who changes and then changes those around her."

For students to understand the significance of the two women's actions, they must be aware of the realities of the segregated South at the time of the Montgomery boycott in 1955. In the warm-up, you can review the ways in which Jim Crow segregation affected people in their daily lives. For the purpose of this film, students should know that not only were seating areas segregated on city buses, but it was against the law for a black and a white person to share the same cab.

If you have time for only a few portions of the film, you might show the opening scene to establish the social context and then proceed to the film's turning point. As the film starts, Odessa (played by Whoopi Goldberg) comes into the kitchen to begin work while the Thompson family is getting ready for the day. Miriam (played by Sissy Spacek) seems very much the socialite housewife, preoccupied with preparations for a cocktail party she is giving that evening. Her older daughter is looking for her tennis racket, and her husband is concerned with his golf clubs. As Odessa cleans up, there is little interaction between her and the others except for some brief instructions from Miriam.

In the scene which marks the film's turning point, the two women have a genuine conversation, perhaps for the first time. Miriam has been driving Odessa to work several days a week during the bus boycott, not out of a sympathetic political conviction, but as a practical solution to her own problem: she needs a housekeeper, and she drives out near Odessa's home anyway to go to market. When her husband finds out, however, he is enraged and insists that she stop. That day Odessa walks nine miles through pouring rain, arriving drenched at the Thompsons' home. Rather than maintain her normal silence, hiding her true feelings, Odessa steps out of her prescribed role and asks, "Miss Thompson, why did you call me at home and tell me you couldn't carry me to work any more?"

This question leads to an extraordinary exchange between the two women. Miriam, obviously embarrassed and uncomfortable, admits that it was not her decision and tries to explain her husband's behavior: "Norman's just always been where everything's segregated, that's just the way he thinks." While she lets Odessa know that this is not the way she herself feels, she says that there is little she can do as a wife. "Years ago I decided I'd live with Norman for the rest of my life," she says. But Odessa knows this is not all there is to Miriam. By the end of the conversation, Odessa says aloud what she really thinks, giving Miriam the courage to distinguish between the woman her husband wants her to be and who she really is.

The film is beautifully crafted, revealing in small details the bond that develops between the two women and the intensity of their emotions. Viewing the entire film will allow students to appreciate the path each woman must travel to reach her decision. Miriam's ultimate defiance of her white world by driving in a car pool to support the boycott might seem rash and surprising to her husband, but to the viewer it represents the decision of a woman who has examined her deepest convictions.

The film received highly favorable reviews, earning the respect of black critics as well as white. In her nationally syndicated column, Coretta Scott King praised the film as one of a few Hollywood productions to do justice to the black freedom struggle.

She says that it "captures the feel of the segregated south of the 1950s," missing on only a few minor points. It overdoes the level of support white women gave the protesters, she says, and the climactic scene at the car-pool headquarters was not historically correct. "It didn't happen quite that way in Montgomery, but similar incidents did occur in other campaigns of the civil rights movement," King says.

What King especially likes about the film is that its main characters are not prominent leaders of the bus boycott but average citizens. Because of this, she says, the film "better portrays the experience of the community."[1] This idea of portraying the community, of showing the average person making everyday decisions, is important in intercultural education. While individually we can only take responsibility for our own actions, we nonetheless all affect each other in ways we cannot know or predict.

Tips for Use: *The Long Walk Home*
Write a script for a dialogue between Odessa and her husband after Odessa returns home from Christmas Day at the Thompsons'.

Who in this film would you most like to have a conversation with and why? What would you like to say to the person, and what do you imagine the reaction might be?

Working through the Law

While the four films discussed above focus on individuals who cross over boundaries to join with individuals on a personal level, other films describe more comprehensive efforts to eliminate discrimination through the law. Indeed, goodwill and humanitarian impulses can only go so far if the system of laws divides people along racial, ethnic, or religious lines. In a number of excellent films which document legal campaigns against discrimination, we see hope for the future in the struggle of dedicated people to ensure human rights and equality for people of all cultural and ethnic backgrounds.

The first of these films, entitled *The Road to Brown*, tells the fascinating but little-known account of black lawyer Charles Hamilton Houston's lifelong battle to end Jim Crow segregation. Houston's inspired legal strategy and his determination to succeed despite tremendous odds make for a gripping story. The documentary first traces the history of segregation since slavery, reviewing landmark cases such as *Dred Scott* and *Plessy v. Ferguson*, and then it focuses on Houston himself. In 1920, when Houston entered Harvard Law School, there were fewer than one hundred black lawyers in the entire South. Appointed dean of the Howard University Law School in 1929, he soon began to put into practice his self-stated philosophy that "a lawyer is either a social engineer or he is a parasite on society."

The heart of the documentary is the section entitled "The Strategy Unfolds," in which Houston, as special counsel to the NAACP, realizes that the way to undermine the entire system of Jim Crow is by targeting segregated education. Launching a number of precedent-setting cases, Houston paved the way for Thurgood Marshall and other black jurists to realize his goal. Just four years after Houston's death in 1950, the historic *Brown v. Board of Education* decision to desegregate the schools was handed down. A second film that takes up where the first leaves off is *Separate but Equal*, a four-hour television miniseries, starring Sidney Poitier, which focuses on events leading to Thurgood Marshall's Supreme Court victory in the *Brown v. Board of Education* case.

Both *The Road to Brown* and *Separate but Equal* are filled with excitement and suspense, but both presuppose some familiarity with the history of the period. Thus, it is helpful to review some background material in the warm-up. Students who have a basic familiarity with the events of the time will not fail to be captured by the human drama of the Brown decision or by its monumental importance in United States history. These films show how legal decisions affect lives, how courtroom rulings can become expressions of a people's highest ideals.

A different side of the struggle for social justice through the law is seen in the video entitled *Seeking Justice: The Story of the Southern Poverty Law Center*. It traces the courageous—and overwhelmingly successful—efforts of this private Alabama organization over the past two decades to "aid the powerless whose human and civil rights have been violated." As defined in the film, the group's weapon is the law, its battlefield is the courtroom, and its enemy is racial and economic injustice.

Though the Southern Poverty Law Center has taken on many cases, it has become known primarily for its uncompromising stand against the Ku Klux Klan. Its bold and successful approach has been to charge the leaders of the Klan for members' actions and sue them for damages as part of a strategy to bankrupt the organization. The Law Center's first encounter with the Klan was in 1979, when it won federal criminal convictions of ten top Klan leaders. Two years later, the center obtained an injunction against the Klan when AKIA (A Klansman I Am) members moved in to destroy the livelihoods of Vietnamese fishermen on the Texas Gulf coast. In retaliation for the center's work, the Klan firebombed its headquarters in 1983, but the work against the Klan continued unabated in a newly rebuilt facility. In 1987, the center obtained a $7-million judgment in favor of Beulah Mae Donald, whose son was lynched by members of the United Klans of America. Today, the organization Klanwatch, founded by the center in 1981, carefully monitors the activities of the Klan, gathering information for legal action through its extensive network of informants.

Interviews with cofounder Morris Dees, legal director Richard Cohen, and clients represented by the center bring the legal cases to life. An emotional interview with Dees, in which he describes the closing argument in the case of Beulah Mae Donald, shows him as a man of enormous commitment and compassion. The lawyers at the center also emerge as dedicated, hardworking idealists who have not only stood their ground against formidable opponents, but have won significant victories.

The work of the center is inspiring, for students can see how it is possible, in an atmosphere of fear and intimidation, to work to protect people from crimes of intolerance. Especially with the reported increases around the country in racial and ethnic violence, it is important for students to see what kinds of effective actions are being taken.

Tips for Use: *Seeking Justice*
The Civil Rights Memorial, created by Maya Lin (architect of the Vietnam Veterans Memorial) was erected in 1989 by the Southern Poverty Law Center (SPLC). Find out more about the memorial and the forty martyrs it honors, and describe your reactions to its design and purpose.

Obtain a copy of the SPLC's new publication, *Teaching Tolerance*. What do you think of this effort to reach teachers and students?

Obtain statistics and information from your local police about hate crimes in your area. Analyze and interpret these statistics in an attempt to explain why these particular crimes may be occurring.

Find out about organizations in your area, like Klanwatch, that are working to fight racism and prejudice. Gather pertinent literature and invite speakers to class.

Contact the Southern Poverty Law Center (400 Washington Ave., Montgomery, AL 36104) to find out how you might lend support.

Further Reading
A Season for Justice, Morris Dees with Steve Fiffer (New York: Macmillan, 1991).

Crosscurrents in the Arts

The arts offer a very different way of bringing cultures together. While the arts have long been recognized as having universal appeal, a true appreciation of art in any culture, including one's own, does not come easily. Nonetheless, the potential of art, particularly music, dance, and painting, to reach across boundaries is extraordinary.

A remarkable example of this potential is seen in *Kembali—To Return*, which shows how music connects people from Oakland, California, with a culture 10,000 miles away on the Indonesian island of Bali. In Oakland, an ensemble of thirty musicians and dancers has dedicated itself for the past six years to rehearsing— and performing across the United States—the captivating musical form of the Balinese gamelan. The word "gamelan" refers to the orchestra itself, which consists primarily of tuned metal or wooden chimes and other percussion instruments. The gamelan is re-nowned for its tonal range and sophisticated rhythms, featuring quickly shifting tempos, and one can easily believe the Oakland musicians' claim that they practice and perform simply because they love the music.

The story begins when the governor of Bali invites the group to perform at the Annual Balinese Arts Festival. *Kembali* traces this unusual journey, the first American performances of Balinese music and dance for the Balinese. As the members of the group, many of whom have never been to Bali, arrive on the island and are exposed to its sights and sounds, the viewers of the documentary are also given a fascinating glimpse of the rich culture. We visit a shop where musical instruments are made by hand, observe a dance class, and watch master musicians as they help the Americans rehearse. Through all this, we begin to see, along with the musicians, how music is an expression of Balinese culture and tightly interwoven with daily life.

The high points of the film, of course, are the actual musical performances. After a week of feverish practice, the group travels to a village in the north for its first performance at a local concert. The fact that the Americans are scheduled to follow one of the finest gamelans in Bali only increases their nervousness. Though aware of the other group's reputation, the Americans are not prepared for its brilliance. As they watch a nine-year-old boy's "spellbinding dance," members of the Oakland ensemble wonder if their own performance "could ever capture any of the same magic." By this time we, as viewers, are also nervous, wondering how our fellow Americans will do. That their opening chord is met with spontaneous applause from an appreciative audience is a great relief. After the performance, which is judged a success, members of the ensemble express surprise at the degree of audience response; unlike American audiences unfamiliar with the music, the Balinese applaud often when they are pleased or break into gales of laughter at something incorrect or unexpected. It seems that the audience in turn is surprised by the female members of the group, something quite rare in Bali.

Anticipation has again reached a high pitch by the evening of the final performance at the art and music festival, which is featuring the Americans in solo performance televised to the entire island. To a packed hall, with the governor in the front row, the group performs its repertoire of five classical pieces, followed by one original composition, a humorous mix of Balinese music with tap, body music, and vaudeville. Although the audience clearly appreciate and enjoy the traditional pieces, the innovative final selection captures their imagination. Their enthusiastic response far exceeds the Americans' expectations; in hindsight, however, the narrator sees it as fitting that the "blending of Western and Balinese forms...turned out to be the most popular."

In classroom analysis, you might begin by asking students their responses to the performances. How did they react to the Balinese music and dance? To the sounds themselves? To the asymmetry of the dance? To the colors and costumes? Also, how did they feel about the Americans performing this type of music? Have the students ever tried anything like this themselves? How did it feel? What did they learn from their efforts?

If anyone in the class is able to demonstrate an art form from another culture, this is a marvelous opportunity to explore the themes raised in the film. In a course I recently took on intercultural communication, a class member was able to teach the rest of us a few basic steps of Balinese dance. The difficulty we all had placing our feet in asymmetrical stances and shifting our eyes gave us not only added appreciation for the art form itself, but also a glimpse into the different worldview it expresses.

You might wish to explore further the idea, touched on briefly in the film, of how Balinese music is an expression of their culture and worldview. How are, in the narrator's words, the "borders between arts, religion, and daily life" blurred for the Balinese? Do the arts have a similar role in our culture? How does Balinese music reflect a deep sense of harmony and community? How is this different from the spirit conveyed by Western music? Students can try to compare what they observed in the film with the way we learn music, practice music, and incorporate it into our lives.

The film leaves us with a sense of the exhilarating effect of mixing cultures, of cross-fertilization. While the Americans can never master gamelan music as do the Balinese, they nonetheless make it a part of themselves. As their original composition demonstrates, they also bring something of themselves to it, creating a form which the Balinese themselves recognize as noteworthy. Furthermore, they demonstrate goodwill and respect for another culture by their own love for its music and dedication to it.

Creating Community

In the inspiring film *Chicano Park*, the arts play a different role, giving a disenfranchised ethnic group a means of empowerment and self-expression. The documentary traces the history of Barrio Logan, a Mexican-American community just south of downtown San Diego and seventeen miles from the Mexican border. Flourishing and attractive in the 1920s, the neighborhood by the 1950s was threatened by Interstate 5, the Coronado Bridge, and proliferating junkyards. Rather than moving out or giving in to the blight and decay imposed upon them by a growing San Diego, the residents mobilized in 1970 and created Chicano Park in the heart of the barrio.

The film shows how for the next twenty years the park became the focus of the residents' efforts to keep their community alive and vital. Musicians, muralists, and community leaders explain how the struggle took shape and what it meant to them. This struggle was, on the one hand, a political one, as the community gradually gained the courage and ability to defend itself against powerful forces in city government. But the real story of Barrio Logan is the community's striving for its identity through artistic expression. Amazingly, the cumbersome freeway pillars cutting through the park became backdrops for giant murals, giving artists an opportunity to discover "where we came from and where we are going as a people." As one muralist says, we "exploded on the walls," celebrating all the images from the Chicano experience. Another artist explains, "We write our history for ourselves and paint it on our murals."

The murals photographed in the film are extraordinary, offering eloquent testimony to this community's creativity and pride in its heritage. Famous throughout the Southwest, Chicano Park is an example to all communities of the strength and beauty which can emerge from people joining together.

For Chicano students, the film is important as part of their recent history. All other students will undoubtedly be captured by the powerful images of the murals and the undaunted spirit of the residents. You might begin discussion by asking students about their impressions of the murals. What did they like or dislike? What seemed new or different to them? What questions did the murals raise in their minds? What would they like to know more about? You will especially want to discuss with students how their stereotypes of Chicanos are contradicted by the residents of Barrio Logan.

A Love of Learning

The final example here of successfully crossing cultures has to do with teaching and learning. When Mark Salzman, a 1982 Yale graduate in Chinese language and literature, embarked for China after graduation, his purpose was to teach English. His subsequent book, *Iron And Silk*,[2] and his movie with the same title, document both his experiences as a teacher and, more importantly, as an avid student of China. His love for the culture and desire to learn at every opportunity are so genuine that they capture our interest as well, even if we have never thought about trying calligraphy or the martial arts as he does.

In his 1991 film, Salzman plays himself in a script which follows the book in basic format. Unfortunately, the charm of the book does not quite translate onto the screen, and the author's romance with a young Chinese woman is given a cinematic inflation at the expense of much more interesting encounters between Salzman and other Chinese people described in the book. Nevertheless, the film is a unique example of how captivating the study of another culture can be.

The film opens with Salzman's arrival by train at Hangzhou, where he is greeted by officials from Hangzhou Teachers' College. His assignment, to teach advanced English to a group of "middle-aged English teachers," is explored in classroom scenes spread through the film. Each scene captures something of the complexity and poignancy of life in China, in particular when the Chinese students read their essays on "My Happiest Moment." What becomes evident from these encounters is that while "Teacher Mark" is helping his students learn more about English and America, he is at the same time their student, learning from them invaluable lessons about China.

For Salzman, it seems that all of China is a classroom. Having studied martial arts since he was a child, he entreats Pan Qingfu, a legendary champion in martial arts, to take him on as a pupil. Rising for 6:00 A.M. lessons and spending the recommended four to six hours a day practicing are no deterrent to Salzman. He wants to capture the spirit of *wushu* (martial arts) and prove to Pan that he can "eat bitter."

Although learning wushu is Salzman's primary interest in the film, we also see him as he works with Teacher Wei, who is assigned to him by the college, to improve his Chinese. Salzman speaks both English and Mandarin in the film, impressing viewers with his facility in the foreign language. Teacher Wei, however, is not so easily impressed and insists that he master his characters. She also teaches him about social propriety, letting him know gently but firmly when he makes mistakes. Their first lesson, for example, is a wonderful cross-cultural encounter in which she guides him through the intricacies of polite behavior. She first reminds him that he cannot jump right into the writing task for the day, for "in China, when someone visits you in your home, you always offer them tea and something to eat first." Salzman quickly offers tea, which she accepts, but she turns down his offer of candy. He asks why she requested it if she didn't want it, but she says she didn't request it; she merely told him he must offer it. When he goes to put it away, she says no, he musn't put it away, but must offer it again. Similarly, Salzman learns that he must persist in accompanying Teacher Wei home, at least a good part of the way, despite her protest that he has walked far enough. As Mark says, "With Teacher Wei, I was never sure when the lesson was over."

In class discussions of *Iron and Silk*, you can focus on what makes Salzman such a good learner. What is it about his attitude that allows him to enter another culture as different from his as the Chinese and actually make it his own? What does he learn from the others? What do they learn from him? Salzman's ability to forge relationships with his students and his teachers so that everyone is enriched serves as an example to all those who believe in the value of crossing cultures.

Tips for Use: *Iron and Silk*

If you were Mark Salzman, what aspects of American culture and society would you most like to present to your Chinese students? What artifacts of American culture would you take with you to China to show to others? What songs would you sing or play? What films would you like to show?

Invite Chinese students or scholars on your campus to give their impressions of the film. If they haven't seen it, invite them to watch it with you.

Films Discussed

1. **Chicano Park,** 1989, 60 mins., color, Cinema Guild.
2. **Indeed I Have Hope,** 1989, 6 mins., color, Foundation for Global Community (Portland, Oregon).
3. **Iron and Silk,** 1991, 94 mins., color.
4. **Kembali—To Return,** 1990, 46 mins., color, Filmakers Library.
5. **The Long Walk Home,** 1990, 98 mins., color.
6. **Neve Shalom/Wahat al-Salam,** 1989, 6 mins., color, Foundation for Global Community (Portland, Oregon).
7. **The Road to Brown,** 1990, 47 mins., color, California Newsreel.
8. **Seeking Justice: The Story of the Southern Poverty Law Center,** 1990, 18 mins., color, Southern Poverty Law Center.
9. **Separate but Equal,** 1991, 194 mins., color, University of Illinois Film/Video Center.
10. **Talking to the Enemy: Voices of Rage and Sorrow,** 1988, 54 mins., color, Filmakers Library.

Related Films

1. **Distant Harmony: Pavarotti in China**
   1987, 85 mins., color, Facets Multimedia Center
   A joyful celebration of the power of art to bring people from East and West together, as demonstrated by world-renowned Italian tenor Luciano Pavarotti's enormously successful 1986 visit to the People's Republic of China. Film skillfully juxtaposes scenes of daily life in China with fragments of both Chinese and Italian opera.

2. **A Great Wall**
   1986, 100 mins., color, Pacific Arts Video
   When Leo Fang's Chinese-American family makes its first trip to visit relatives in the People's Republic of China, opportunities for culture clash abound. A spirit of good-natured curiosity,

open-mindedness, and laughter on all sides makes this encounter from two sides of the ocean successful as well as entertaining.

3. Jacoba: The Heroism of an "Ordinary" Woman
1989, 63 mins., color, Filmakers Library
A remarkable film that attempts to find out more about Jacoba Omvlee, a Dutch woman who risked her life and the lives of her eight children by hiding the Jewish Ten Brink family in her windmill for three years. Filmmaker Joram Ten Brink skillfully combines documentary footage, reenactments of daily life in hiding, and interviews with Jacoba's grandchildren.

4. Made in China: A Search for Roots
1987, 30 mins., color, Filmakers Library
Charming, funny narration by a young Chinese-American woman in search of her past who goes to live with relatives in Beijing. Very imaginative film that is made to resemble a home movie.

5. Maya Angelou: Rainbow in the Clouds
1992, 60 mins., color, PBS Video
Renowned African-American writer Maya Angelou introduces viewers to the Glide Memorial Church in San Francisco, where whites and people of color from widely diverse backgrounds join together in an affirmation of life. A film that celebrates renewal, healing, and hope.

6. Strangers in Good Company
1990, 100 mins., color, First Run/Icarus Films
When eight elderly women, including a Mohawk Indian, a black, a lesbian, and a nun, are stranded in remote northern Quebec for days, they face their desperate situation with courage and humor. A memorable example of how differences seem not to divide, but prove to be sources of strength and friendship.

7. **Weapons of the Spirit**
1986, 91 mins., color/bw, Vision Video/Gateway
Inspiring story of Le Chambon, a Protestant farming village in the mountains of France which became a haven for Jews from 1940 to 1944. Thousands of residents quietly joined together in defiance of the German occupation, safely harboring 5,000 Jews in their homes. The director, Pierre Sauvage, was born and protected in the village. Serves as an important counterweight to the many despairing films of the Holocaust.

Notes

Chapter 2

An Embarrassment of Riches: How to Find
and Evaluate Films

1. Mobility International produces several videos which show how people with disabilities can participate successfully in international exchanges.
2. Esther R. Sinofsky, *Off-Air Videotaping in Education* (New York: R. R. Bowker, 1984),120.
3. Bernard S. Miller, "Defusing Tensions with Film," *The Bulletin of the National Association of Secondary School Principals* (April 1970), 70-71.
4. Kathi Maio, *Feminist in the Dark* (Freedom, CA: Crossing Press, 1988), 36.
5. Ibid., 42-43.
6. Donald Bogle, *Blacks in American Films and Television: An Encyclopedia* (New York and London: Garland Publishing, 1988), 58.
7. Ibid., 60.
8. Ibid., 59.

Chapter 3

How to Use Cross-Cultural Films:
Thoughts on Pedagogy

1. Cornelius Moore, "Africa through African Eyes," in *Library of African Cinema* (pamphlet available from California Newsreel—see Film Distributors for address), 5.
2. Michael Hilger, *The American Indian in Film* (Metuchen, NJ: Scarecrow Press, 1986), 4.
3. Richard A. Lacey, *Seeing with Feeling: Film in the Classroom* (Philadelphia: W. B. Saunders, 1972), 16.
4. Ibid., 17.
5. Ibid., 24.
6. Ibid., 25.
7. For further information, contact: NAFSA: Association of International Educators, 1875 Connecticut Ave., N.W., Suite 1000, Washington, DC 20009-5728 (tel. 202-462-4811); SIETAR International, 733 15th St., NW, Suite 900, Washington, DC 20005-2112 (tel. 202-737-5000); East-West Center, c/o Richard Brislin, Institute of Culture and Communication, Honolulu, HI 96848; Intercultural Communication Institute, 8835 S.W. Canyon Lane, Suite 238, Portland, OR 97225 (tel. 503-297-4622).
8. Frederick Turner, ed., *The Portable North American Indian Reader* (New York: Viking Press, 1974).
9. The anthologies I have found most useful are: Gary Colombo, Robert Cullen, and Bonnie Lisle, eds., *Rereading America* (New York: St. Martin's Press, 1989); Stuart Hirschberg, ed., *One World, Many Cultures* (New York: Macmillan, 1992); Henry and Myrna Knepler, eds., *Crossing Cultures: Readings for Composition* (New York: Macmillan, 1991); Marilyn Smith Layton, ed., *Intercultural Journeys through Reading and Writing* (New York: HarperCollins, 1991); Tom Lewis and Robert Jungman, eds., *On Being Foreign: Culture Shock in Short Fiction* (Yarmouth, ME: Intercultural Press, 1986); John Repp, ed., *How We Live Now: Contemporary Multicultural Literature* (Boston: St. Martin's

Press, 1992); Rick Simonson and Scott Walker, eds., *Multicul-
tural Literacy: Opening the American Mind* (St. Paul, MN:
Graywolf Press, 1988); Carol J. Verburg, ed., *Ourselves among
Others: Cross-Cultural Readings for Writers*, 2nd ed. (Boston: St.
Martin's Press, 1991); Scott Walker, ed., *Stories from the Ameri-
can Mosaic* (St. Paul, MN: Graywolf Press, 1990); and Scott
Walker, ed., *Stories from the Rest of the World* (St. Paul, MN:
Graywolf Press, 1989).

10. James A. Banks, *Teaching Strategies for Ethnic Studies*, 5th ed.
(Boston: Allyn and Bacon, 1991).

11. In *Intercultural Communication: A Reader*, 6th ed., edited by
Larry A. Samovar and Richard E. Porter (Belmont, CA:
Wadsworth, 1991), 270-76.

Chapter 4

A *Chairy Tale* and Other Classics

1. Kevin W. Kelley, ed., *The Home Planet* (Reading, MA: Addison-
Wesley, 1988), jacket cover. (Original source of the quotation
from Hoyle unobtainable.)

Chapter 5

Unlearning Stereotypes: New Stories
and Histories Emerge

1. John A. Price, "The Stereotyping of North American Indians
in Motion Pictures," in *The Pretend Indians: Images of Native
Americans in the Movies*, edited by Gretchen M. Bataille and
Charles L. P. Silet (Ames, IA: Iowa State University Press,
1980), 88.

2. Richard A. Oehling, "The Yellow Menace: Asian Images in
American Film," in *The Kaleidoscopic Lens: How Hollywood
Views Ethnic Groups*, edited by Randall M. Miller (Englewood,
NJ: Jerome S. Ozer, 1980), 187.

3. One such example is that of San Francisco Bay Area black
leader Willie Brown, who declined to host the premiere of the

film at the last moment, apparently because his aide was offended by its images (see review, "Home-style Racist Kitsch" by Pat Aufderheide in *In These Times*, February 3-9, 1988.)
4. Rebecca Lieb, "Nazi Hate Movies Continue to Ignite Fierce Passions," *New York Times*, 4 August 1991.
5. Donald Bogle, *Blacks in American Films and Television*, 19.
6. Thomas Cripps, *Slow Fade to Black* (London: Oxford University Press, 1977), 43.

Chapter 6

Speaking Different Languages: Verbal and Nonverbal Communication

1. For further information on the legend, see Américo Pardes's *With His Pistol in His Hand* (Austin, TX: University of Texas Press, 1958).
2. My thanks to John Condon, who gave me the idea to compare these two scenes in a seminar of his I attended in the summer of 1990.

Chapter 7

Great Walls of Difference: The International Arena

1. David K. Shipler, *Arab and Jew: Wounded Spirits in a Promised Land* (New York: Penguin, 1987).
2. Richard Attenborough, *Cry Freedom: A Pictorial Record* (New York: Knopf, 1987), 1.
3. Ibid., 3.
4. Keyan Tomaselli, "The Heroism of an Anti-Hero: Panic in the Streets," in *Library of African Cinema* (pamphlet available from California Newsreel), 27.
5. See Mark Lai Him, Genny Lim, Judy Yung, *Island. Poetry and History of Chinese Immigrants on Angel Island 1910-1940* (Seattle: University of Washington Press, 1980).

6. Jean Marie Ackermann, *Films of a Changing World: A Critical International Guide* vol. 1 (Washington, DC: Society for International Development, 1972), 2.

7. Ibid., 5.

8. Jean Marie Ackermann, *Films of a Changing World: A Critical International Guide* vol. 2 (Washington, DC: Society for International Development, 1976), 56.

9. "Millenium: Not Your Standard Anthropology," in *Oregon Focus Magazine*, 22 May 1992, 10.

Chapter 8

In Our Own Backyard: Cultures within the United States

1. Smith is quoted in Julie Lew, "Hollywood's War on Indians Draws to a Close," *New York Times*, 7 October 1990.

2. Two Elk is quoted in Coretta Scott King, "Yet, 'Dances with Wolves' Dances around Real Issue," *Oregonian*, 5 December 1990.

3. Michael Dorris, "Indians in Aspic," *New York Times*, 29 February 1991.

4. Spike Lee, *Do the Right Thing: A Spike Lee Joint* (New York: Simon and Schuster, 1989), 33.

5. "Do the Right Thing: Issues and Images," *New York Times*, 9 July 1989.

6. Lee, *Do the Right Thing*, 24.

7. Thomas Kochman, *Black and White Styles in Conflict* (Chicago: University of Chicago Press, 1981), 46.

8. Ibid., 43.

9. Jay Carr, "Spike Speaks," *Oregonian*, 9 June 1991.

10. Henry Louis Gates, Jr., " 'Jungle Fever' Charts Black Middle-Class Angst," *New York Times*, 23 June 1991.

11. Karen Grigsby Bates, "They've Gotta Have Us: Hollywood's Black Directors," *New York Times Magazine*, 14 July 1991.

12. Richard Bernstein, "Hollywood Seeks White Audience for Black Films," *New York Times*, 17 July 1991.
13. My sincere appreciation to Shelley Lieberman, Director of Educational Outreach at Griggs Productions, for her assistance and thoughtful suggestions, particularly with regard to the sequencing of the films.

Chapter 9

Studying and Working Abroad: Tales of Adaptation

1. John C. Condon, *With Respect to the Japanese* (Yarmouth, ME: Intercultural Press, 1984).

Chapter 10

Indeed I Have Hope: Succeeding across Cultures

1. Coretta Scott King, " 'Long Walk Home' True Look at Past," *Oregonian*, 15 May 1991.
2. Mark Salzman, *Iron and Silk* (New York: Vintage Books, 1987).

Selected Bibliography

A. Works on Film and Culture

Abrash, Barbara, and Catherine Egan, eds. *Mediating History: The MAP Guide to Independent Video by and about African American, Asian American, Latino, and Native American People*. New York: New York University Press, 1992.

Ackermann, Jean Marie. *Films of a Changing World: A Critical International Guide*, 2 vols. Washington, DC: Society for International Development, 1972, 1976.

Bataille, Gretchen M., and Charles L. P. Silet. *Images of American Indians on Film: An Annotated Bibliography*. New York: Garland Publishing, 1985.

_____, eds. *The Pretend Indians: Images of Native Americans in the Movies*. Ames, IA: Iowa State University Press, 1980.

Baxter, James, and Deena Levine. "Review Article on 'Crosstalk.'" In *Tesol Quarterly* 16, no. 2 (1982), 245-53.

Bogle, Donald. *Blacks in American Films and Television: An Encyclopedia*. New York: Garland Publishing, 1988.

_____. *Toms, Coons, Mulattoes, Mammies and Bucks: An Interpretive History of Blacks in American Films.* New York: Viking, 1973.

Bourne, St. Clair. "The African Image in American Cinema." In *Black Scholar* 21, no. 2 (March/April/May 1990), 13-19.

Cham, Mybe B., and Claire Andrade Watkins, eds. *Blackframes: Critical Perspectives on Black Independent Cinema.* Cambridge: The MIT Press, 1988.

Condon, John. "Exploring Intercultural Communication through Literature and Film." *World Englishes,* vol. 5, no. 2/3 (1986): 153-61.

Cortes, Carlos E., and Leon G. Campbell. *Race and Ethnicity in the History of the Americas: A Filmic Approach.* Riverside: University of California, 1979.

_____. "Empowerment through Media Literacy: A Multicultural Approach." In *Empowerment through Multicultural Education.* Albany: State University of New York Press, 1991.

Costner, Kevin, Michael Blake, and Jim Wilson. *Dances with Wolves: The Illustrated Story of the Epic Film.* New York: Newmarket Press, 1990.

Cripps, Thomas. *Slow Fade to Black: The Negro in American Film, 1900-1942.* London: Oxford University Press, 1977.

Erens, Patricia. *The Jew in American Cinema.* Bloomington: University of Indiana Press, 1984.

Friar, Ralph, and Natasha Friar. *The Only Good Indian...The Hollywood Gospel.* New York: Drama Book Specialists, 1972.

Friedman, Lester D. *The Jewish Image in American Film*. Secaucus, NJ: Citadel Press, 1987.

Garrity, Henry A. *Film in the French Classroom*. Cambridge, MA: Polyglot, 1987.

Gee, Bill J., ed. *Asian-American Media Reference Guide*. 2d ed. New York: Asian CineVision, 1990.

Grilli, Peter, ed. *Japan in Film*. New York: Japan Society, 1984.

Hadley-Garcia, George. *Hispanic Hollywood: The Latins in Motion Pictures*. New York: Carol Publishing, 1990.

Hilger, Michael. *The American Indian in Film*. Metuchen, NJ: Scarecrow Press, 1986.

Hyatt, Marshall. *The Afro-American Cinematic Experience: An Annotated Bibliography and Filmography*. Wilmington, DE: Scholarly Resources, 1983.

Keller, Gary D. *Chicano Cinema*. New York: Bilingual Review/ Press, 1985.

Klotman, Phyllis Rauch. *Frame by Frame: A Black Filmography*. Bloomington: Indiana University Press, 1979.

Lacey, Richard A. *Seeing with Feeling: Film in the Classroom*. Philadelphia: W. B. Saunders, 1972.

Lee, Spike. *Do the Right Thing: A Spike Lee Joint*. New York: Simon and Schuster, 1989.

Leong, Russell, ed. *Moving the Image: Independent Asian-Pacific-American Media Arts*. Los Angeles: UCLA Asian-American Studies Center, 1991.

Lippitt, Phyllis, and Gordon Lippitt. "Use of Non-verbal Films as Stimulus for Learning." In *Helping across Cultures*, edited by Gordon L. Lippitt and David S. Hoopes, 33-36. Washington, DC: International Consultants Foundation, 1978.

Loukides, Paul, and Linda K. Fuller, eds. *Beyond the Stars: Stock Characters in American Popular Film*. Bowling Green, OH: Bowling Green State University Popular Press, 1990.

Miller, Randall M., ed. *The Kaleidoscopic Lens: How Hollywood Views Ethnic Groups*. Englewood, NJ: Jerome S. Ozer, 1980.

Noriega, Chon A., ed. *Chicanos and Film: Essays on Chicano Representation and Resistance*. New York: Garland Publishing, 1992.

Ramsey, Sheila, and Toby S. Frank. "Suggestions for the Discussion of Films—Example: 'A Chairy Tale.'" In *Multicultural Education: A Cross-Cultural Training Approach*, edited by Margaret D. Pusch, 201-03. Yarmouth, ME: Intercultural Press, 1979.

Shapiro, Howard. "Suggestions for Improving Film Discussions." In *Beyond Experience*, edited by Donald Batchelder and Elizabeth G. Warner, 75-77. Brattleboro, VT: The Experiment Press, 1977.

Weatherford, Elizabeth, and Emilia Seubert, eds. *Native Americans on Film and Video*, 2 vols. New York: Museum of the American Indian, 1981, 1987.

Woll, Allen L. *The Latin Image in American Film*. Los Angeles: UCLA Latin-American Center Publications, 1977.

Wong, Eugene Franklin. *On Visual Media Racism: Asians in the American Motion Pictures*. New York: Arno Press, 1978.

Zeigler, Lee. *Film and Video Resources for International Educational Exchange*. Washington, DC: NAFSA: Assn. of Int'l Educators, 1992.

B. Reference Works

Bowker's Complete Video Directory 1992, 2 vols. New Providence, NJ: R. R. Bowker, 1992.

Educational Film and Video Locator, 2 vols., 4th ed. New York: R. R. Bowker, 1990-91.

Lyon, Christopher, ed. *International Dictionary of Films and Filmmakers*, 2 vols. Chicago: St. James Press, 1990.

Magill, Frank N., ed. *Magill's Cinema Annual*. Englewood Cliffs, NJ: Salem Press.

Magill, Frank N., ed. *Magill's Survey of Cinema*, 21 vols. Englewood Cliffs, NJ: Salem Press.

New York Times Film Reviews. New York: *New York Times*.

Ozer, Jerome S., ed. *Film Review Annual*. Englewood, NJ: Jerome S. Ozer.

Thomas, Nicolas, ed. *International Directory of Films and Filmmakers*, 2 vols. Chicago: St. James Press, 1990-91.

Variety's Film Reviews. New Providence, NJ: R. R. Bowker.

Wakeman, John, ed. *World Film Directors*, 2 vols. New York: H. W. Wilson, 1987-88.

Wall, Edward, ed. *Media Review Digest*. Ann Arbor, MI: Pierian Press.

Wynar, Lubomyr R. *Encyclopedic Directory of Ethnic Newspapers and Periodicals in the United States*. Littleton, CO: Libraries Unlimited, 1972.

Film Distributors and Rental Sources

BNA Communications, Inc.
9439 Key West Ave.
Rockville, MD 20850
Tel. (301) 948-0540

California Newsreel
149 Ninth St., Room 420
San Francisco, CA 94103
Tel. (415) 621-6196

Catticus Corporation
2600 10th St.
Berkeley, CA 94710
Tel. (415) 548-0854

Center for New American Media
524 Broadway
New York, NY 10012
Tel. (212) 925-5665
Fax: (212) 925-5692

Cinema Guild
1697 Broadway, Suite 802
New York, NY 10019
Tel. (212) 246-5522
Fax: (212) 246-5525

Coronet/MTI Film and Video
108 Wilmot Rd.
Deerfield, IL 60015
Tel. (708) 940-1260
     (800) 777-2400
Fax: (708) 940-3640

CRM/McGraw Hill Films
2215 Faraday Ave.
Carlsbad, CA 92008
Tel. (619) 431-9800

Encyclopedia Britannica Educational Corp.
310 South Michigan Ave.
Chicago, IL 60604
Tel. (312) 347-7900
     (800) 554-9862
Fax: (312) 347-7903

Facets Multimedia Center
1517 West Fullerton Ave.
Chicago, IL 60614
Tel. (312) 281-9075
     (800) 331-6197
Fax: (312) 929-5437

Filmakers Library
124 East 40th St., Suite 901
New York, NY 10016
Tel. (212) 808-4980
Fax: (212) 808-4983

FilmFair Communications
PO Box 7314
North Hollywood, CA 91603-7314
Tel. (818) 985-0244
Fax: (818)766-8786

Films for the Humanities and Sciences
Box 2053
Princeton, NJ 08543
Tel. (609) 452-1128
Fax: (602) 894-8406

Films, Inc.
5547 North Ravenswood Ave.
Chicago, IL 60640
Tel. (312) 878-2600
     (800) 323-4222
Fax: (312) 878-2895

First Run/Icarus Films
153 Waverly Place, Sixth Floor
New York, NY 10014
Tel. (212) 727-1711
     (800) 876-1710
Fax: (212) 989-7649

Foundation for Global Community/Beyond War
222 High St.
Palo Alto, CA 94301-1097
Tel. (415) 328-7756
Fax: (415) 328-7785

Foundation for Global Community/Beyond War
The Galleria
921 S.W. Morrison, Suite 512
Portland, OR 97205
Tel. (503) 295-1121

Griggs Productions, Inc.
302 23rd Ave.
San Francisco, CA 94121
Tel. (415) 668-4200
Fax. (415) 668-6004

Home Film Festival
PO Box 2032
Scranton , PA 18501
Tel. (800) 258-3456

Indiana University Center for Media and Teaching Resources
Indiana University
Bloomington, Indiana 47405-5901
Tel. (812) 855-8087
    (800) 942-0481 (in Indiana)
    (800) 552-8620 (out of state)
Fax: (812) 855-8404

Intercultural Press, Inc.
PO Box 700
Yarmouth, ME 04096
Tel. (207) 846-5168
Fax: (207) 846-5181

Intercultural Relations Institute
2439 Birch St., Suite 8
Palo Alto, CA 94306

Intercultural Training Resources, Inc. (ITRI)
200 Clocktower Place, Suite B-205
Carmel, CA 93923
Tel. (408) 626-2035
      (800) 626-2047
Fax: (408) 626-8932

International Film Bureau, Inc.
332 S. Michigan Ave.
Chicago, IL 60604-4382
Tel. (312) 427-4545
      (800) 432-2241

Maryknoll World Productions
Media Relations
Maryknoll, NY 10545
Tel. (800) 227-8523

Mobility International USA
PO Box 3551
Eugene, OR 97403
Tel. (503) 343-1284

NAATA/CrossCurrent Media
346 9th St., 2nd Floor
San Francisco, CA 94103
Tel. (415) 552-9550
Fax: (415) 863-7428

NAFSA: Association of International Educators
1875 Connecticut Ave., N.W.
Suite 1000
Washington, DC 20009-5728
Tel. (202) 462-4811

National Film Board of Canada
1251 Avenue of the Americas, 16th Floor
New York, NY 10020
Tel. (212) 586-5131
Fax: (212) 575-2382

New Day Films
121 W. 27th St., Suite 902
New York, NY 10001
Tel. (212) 645-8210

Northeast Conference Media
PO Box 623
Middlebury, VT 05753

Pacific Arts Video
11858 La Grange Ave.
Los Angeles, CA 90025
Tel. (310) 820-0991

PBS Video
1320 Braddock Place
Alexandria, VA 22314-1698
Tel. (800) 344-3337
Fax: (703) 739-5269

Phoenix/BFA Films and Video
468 Park Ave., S.
New York, NY 10016
Tel. (212) 684-5910
    (800) 221-1274

Portland State University Continuing Education Film and
Video Library
1633 S.W. Park Ave.
PO Box 1383
Portland , OR 97207
Tel. (503) 464-4890
    (800) 452-4909 ext. 4890 (Oregon)
    (800) 547-8887 ext. 4890 (out of state)

Pyramid Film and Video
PO Box 1048
Santa Monica, CA
Tel. (310) 828-7577
    (800) 421-2304
Fax: (213) 453-9083

Southern Poverty Law Center
400 Washington Ave.
Montgomery, AL 36104

Sterling Educational Films, Inc.
241 E. 34th St.
New York, NY 10016

Syracuse University Rental Center
1455 East Colvin St.
Syracuse, NY 13244-5150
Tel. (315) 423-2452
     (800) 345-6797 (New York)
     (800) 223-2409 (out of state)

Tamarelle's
7900 Hickman Road
Des Moines, IA 50322
Tel. (515) 254-7253
     (800) 356-3577
Fax: (515) 254-7021

Third World Newsreel
335 West 38th St., 5th Floor
New York, NY 10018
Tel. (212) 947-9277

UNICEF Headquarters
Division of Information
Chief, Radio/TV/Film Section
UNICEF House
3 United Nations Plaza
New York, NY 10017

United Nations
Department of Public Information
Dissemination Division
Room S-805 A
UN Plaza
New York, NY 10017
Tel. (212) 963-6982
Fax: (212) 963-6869

University of California Extension Media Center (UCEMC)
2176 Shattuck Ave.
Berkeley, CA 94704
Tel. (510) 642-0460

University of Illinois Film/Video Center
1325 S. Oak St.
Champaign, IL 61820
Tel. (217) 333-1360
　　(800) 252-1357 (Illinois)
　　(800) 367-3456 (out of state)

University of Minnesota Film and Video Service
1313 5th St. S.E., Suite 108
Minneapolis, MN 55414
Tel. (800) 542-0013 (Minnesota)
　　(800) 847-8251 (out of state)
Fax: (612) 627-4280

University of Washington Instructional Media Services
35-D Kane Hall DG-10
University of Washington
Seattle, WA 98195
Tel. (206) 543-9909

Vision Video/ Gateway
2030 Wentz Church Rd., Box 540
Worcester, PA 19490
Tel. (215) 584-1893
    (800) 523-0226

Women Make Movies
225 Lafayette St., Suite 206
New York, NY 10012
Tel. (212) 925-0606
Fax: (212) 925-2052

Film Index

A

B

J

K

L

M